THE
CHICANO
HERITAGE

HENRY B. GONZALEZ

A Political Profile

Eugene Rodriguez, Jr.

ARNO PRESS

A New York Times Company

New York — 1976

Editorial Supervision: LESLIE PARR

———•———

First publication in book form, 1976
  by Arno Press Inc.

Copyright © 1976 by Eugene Rodriguez, Jr.

THE CHICANO HERITAGE
ISBN for complete set: 0-405-09480-9
See last pages of this volume for titles.

Manufactured in the United States of America

———•———

Library of Congress Cataloging in Publication Data

Rodriguez, Eugene, 1941-
  Henry B. Gonzalez : a political profile.

  (The Chicano heritage)
  Originally presented as the author's thesis
(M.A.), St. Mary's University, San Antonio, Tex.,
1965.
  1. Gonzalez, Henry Barbosa, 1916-   I. Series.
E840.8.G63R6 1976   328.73'092'4 [B]   76-1568
ISBN 0-405-09522-8

HENRY B. GONZALEZ: A POLITICAL PROFILE

A

THESIS

Presented to the Faculty of the Graduate School of

St. Mary's University in Partial Fulfillment

of the Requirements

For the Degree of

MASTER OF ARTS

in

Government

By

Eugene Rodriguez, Jr.

San Antonio, Texas

May, 1965

FOREWORD

Over ten years have passed since the writing of this work. During this period, significant events have transpired not only in the public life of Henry B. Gonzalez, but in the political history of the nation. We have, for example, experienced the enthusiastic initiatives of the Great Society, the turmoil of the Vietnam conflict and the shocking revelations of Watergate. All of these experiences have affected the standards we place on our public officials.

Certainly there is a need to examine the public performance of Henry B. Gonzalez in the light of these expectations. While I hope to complete this major undertaking in the near future, some recent facts and observations are provided in the Epilogue. Although all important considerations are not reflected, some events and facts are identified that should help interpret Gonzalez' career in the light of politics in the late sixties and early seventies.

No changes have been made to the original text except for a handful of factual corrections or clarifications. I am grateful to Gail Beagle, Executive Assistant to Gonzalez for helping identify the factual errors and suggesting appropriate corrections which preserved the original style and content.

One significant point that should be mentioned at this time is the use of the term "Latin American" throughout the text. This reflects the fact that "Mexican American" and "Chicano" were not yet in the domain of common usage in 1965. When you read the text, please keep this in mind and substitute the term you feel most comfortable using.

Finally, I want to thank Arno Press and Professor Carlos E. Cortes for the opportunity to share this work with others who have an interest in the lives and works of Mexican Americans who have achieved significant places in the nation's history. It is particularly meaningful that this work is being published during the Bicentennial year. One way of learning more about ourselves is to know about the public leaders we elect to represent us. I trust, therefore, that in reading the political profile of Henry B. Gonzalez, you will gain new insights into your own.

Eugene Rodriguez, Jr.
San Antonio, Texas, 1976

PREFACE

The impact of U.S. Representative Henry B. Gonzalez on the
local, state, and national political arenas has been impressive and
real. Not only have his pioneering exploits stimulated the political
emergence of a great number of Americans of Mexican descent, but also
his political and legislative accomplishments have been widely recognized and reported by the national press. Although he has been the
subject of several newspaper and periodical articles and editorials,
there has not been a thorough political profile written about him.
For this reason, in addition to a series of favorable circumstances
that prompted me, I decided to conduct a study of the political life
of Congressman Gonzalez.

This is not a biography of the whole man, but a profile of his
political career. The study is limited to those environmental influences that are considered to have significantly contributed to his
political development. The political experience Gonzalez acquired
while in local and state elected offices is treated in a manner that
will attempt to illustrate particular qualities and tenets that have
influenced his performance in office. As a member of Congress he has
been called upon to test and utilize these characteristics. It is my
contention that Gonzalez has emerged successfully in politics because
of a unique pattern of development.

In my research, I found it beneficial to interview individuals
with personal, family, and political knowledge and opinions about
Gonzalez. In some instances I do not refer to the interviewee by name

but by some descriptive phrase. This was simply a discretionary decision by mutual agreement with the interviewee. The use of the terms, "Latin American" and "Anglo," can be confusing to those unfamiliar with life in the Southwest. For this reason I have defined the terms in the text or in footnotes.

I owe thanks and appreciation to a multitude of people. I am especially grateful to Congressman Gonzalez for graciously consenting to my undertaking this work, for his willing cooperation in many discussions, and for allowing me complete freedom and access to his files, correspondence, and scrapbooks. Members of the congressman's staff—my co-workers—have been particularly helpful in offering their knowledge, insights, and encouragements. My special thanks must go to the members of the Department of Government of St. Mary's University, particularly to my adviser, Dr. Bill Crane. Without his understanding patience and helpful encouragement, it is doubtful that this study would have been completed.

It has been difficult for me to avoid bias in preparation of this work. As a member of the congressman's staff and as a long-time supporter and admirer of his, I must admit my partisanship. However, I have tried to be objective.

May, 1965   E. R., Jr.

TABLE OF CONTENTS

CHAPTER I

AN INTRODUCTION TO SAN ANTONIO, TEXAS

It is well noted that the American Revolution has many sons and daughters who take pride in relating the honorable history of their forebearers. Much like the American Revolution, San Antonio has many sons and daughters--some native, others adopted--who point with pride to its memorable and unique past; and, they do so with good reason.

Although historians are not in agreement as to the exact year in which the Spanish first visited the site of the present city, there is unanimity in the belief that San Antonio's San Pedro Springs provided water for an Indian community long before a Spaniard quenched his thirst with their refreshing waters. Some advance the theory that in 1535 Cabeza de Vaca sighted an Indian settlement where San Antonio now stands, thereby distinguishing the city as the oldest identifiable community in the United States.[1] This is but one of many characteristics that its sons and daughters point to in boasting of the "uniqueness" of San Antonio.

---

[1] Carlos E. Castañeda, Our Catholic Heritage in Texas, 1519-1936, I: The Mission Era: The Finding of Texas, 1519-1693 (Austin: Von Boeckmann-Jones Co., 1936), 75.

The name San Antonio was first associated with the location of
the present city in 1691 when a Spanish expedition led by Don Domingo
Teran de los Rios, Governor of Coahuila, a northern province of Mexico,
and first governor of the frontier province of Texas, paused at an
Indian village called Yanaguana at the headwaters of a river he named
San Antonio de Padua. Father Damian Massanet, who accompanied Teran,
was impressed by the natural beauty of the site and, coincidentally,
called it San Antonio de Padua whose feast was that day. Later expedi-
tions stopped at the site, including one led by Louis Juchereau de St.
Denis who reported it a likely spot for French settlement.[2]

French involvement in Texas and the proddings of a missionary,
Father Antonio Olivares, prompted the Spanish to establish an outpost
halfway between Monclova, capital of Coahuila, and the missions in outlying East Texas. Thus, in 1718 Martin de Alarcon, new governor of
the province of Texas, set out to establish a mission and a presidio
at the site named by Massanet and Teran. When he arrived he founded
the Mission San Antonio de Valero in honor of the Marquis of Valero,
the Viceroy of Mexico, and then set up the presidio in the settlement
he named Villa de Bexar in honor of the Viceroy's brother, the Duke of
Bexar.[3]

---

[2]Ibid., II, 365.

[3]Charles Ramsdell, San Antonio (Austin: The University of
Texas Press, 1959), p. 15.

In 1722 the Marquis San Miguel de Aguayo arrived with cavalry and reinforced the presidio which was now called San Antonio de Bexar. He believed that success of Spanish claims on Texas depended on civil settlements and requested that 400 families be brought to the San Antonio area. However, only sixteen families arrived in 1731. These were Canary Islanders who were given land near the fort and who called their settlement San Fernando. It is recorded that the settlers were not happy in their new surroundings and were given to much quarrelling among themselves and with the inhabitants of the missions. There were, by that time, five missions in the area wherein priests ministered to the Indians.[4]

By the turn of the century peace had been made with the troublesome Apaches and Comanches, and Spanish soldiers of the presidio were then occupied with the protection of outlying areas from aggressive Americans who were continually exploring the possibilities in Texas. One of these Americans was Zubulon Pike, an Army officer, who, though a captive, was treated royally in San Antonio and went away favorably impressed.[5]

The Mexican Revolution of 1810 spread into Texas with a band of American adventurers, Mexicans, and Indians battling the Spanish in San Antonio. However, the insurgents were defeated in 1813 and the

[4]Ibid., pp. 22-28.

[5]Ibid., p. 30.

city declined in population and importance. Mexico finally won its independence in 1821 and a new era was born.

Americans, led by Stephen F. Austin, moved into Texas in 1821 after obtaining permission from the new government of Mexico. By 1835 they had gained enough strength to join with disenchanted Mexicans in revolt against the Mexican dictator, Santa Anna. Several battles were fought in San Antonio including the famous encounter at the Alamo where the now immortal band of 182 died under the assault of General Santa Anna. Later the Mexicans were crushed in the Battle of San Jacinto and San Antonio became a part of the Republic of Texas. The city was then twice invaded by Mexican troops, forcing most women and children to remain away until 1845 when Texas joined the United States.

San Antonio began a steady rise in population after Texas entered the Union. A vast number of Germans converged on the city as did many American adventurers. In 1846 the city's population was estimated at 800, but by 1850 it had risen to 3,448 and then to 8,235 in 1860.[6]

Just prior to the Civil War two memorable historical events occurred when General David E. Twiggs surrendered all of the American equipment in Texas to a group of local secessionists and Colonel Robert E. Lee, who was stationed in San Antonio, decided that he owed first allegiance to his native state of Virginia. Despite Governor Sam

---

[6]Ibid., p. 43.

Houston's passionate opposition and almost unanimous dissent among the German settlers, Texas became part of the Confederacy.

Similar to most Southern cities, San Antonio recovered slowly from the Civil War. Cowboys--veterans of the cattle drives--and soldiers--veterans of Indian fights and the Civil War--were the most frequent visitors to the city. Although they delighted in the wide-open atmosphere of San Antonio, even they did not believe the town had a bright future. It was not until 1877 that San Antonio embarked on a meteoric rise. The cause of this success was the railroad which transformed the town from a "rude Spanish outpost to a modern city."[7]

By 1880 San Antonio had become the greatest horse market in the world. Buyers from the world over purchased carloads of horses, many of which had been brought from Mexico. The city was also a center for wool and cotton and the first cement plant west of the Mississippi River was built here around that time. Thousands gained employment in a pecan-shelling industry which supplied the entire country. There was a genuine lure of employment at good pay that brought new citizens to the city. From 1870 to 1890 the population jumped from 12,256 to 37,673. Business was exploding from an annual volume of $10,000,000 in 1886 to a phenomenal $31,000,000 just 4 years later.[8]

---

[7]Ibid., p. 46.

[8]Boyce House, City of Flaming Adventure (San Antonio: The Naylor Company, 1949), pp. 171-173.

San Antonio had finally come into its own by 1891 when it received national recognition with the visit of President Benjamin Harrison. Anxious to impress him, San Antonians planned a "battle of flowers" parade in his honor, but a torrential rain on the day of his visit prevented its presentation. San Antonians have always been noted for their reluctance to pass up any opportunity for a fiesta and, true to their tradition, they held the parade three days later for their own amusement.[9]

At the close of the nineteenth century San Antonio, a prosperous and elegant city, was noted for its free thinking and free drinking. Dixie Williams, a Baptist evangelist, told a San Antonio audience that their city was the "wickedest city in the Union, not excepting Washington City, which is the wickedest out of hell."[10] It is not known if Williams was able to convert any of his audience, but there is much evidence that the rest of the city failed to heed his call. This may be why Teddy Roosevelt felt he could find an ample supply of volunteers in San Antonio for his Rough Riders. Roosevelt trained his men in this city and then led them into battle up San Juan Hill.

The city continued its remarkable rate of growth during the early part of the twentieth century. By 1930 San Antonio had gained 178,000 residents for a 335 per cent increase. Yet, this rate was not

---

[9] Ibid., p. 174.

[10] Federal Writers' Project, Works Progress Administration, San Antonio, An Authoritative Guide to the City and Its Environs ("American Guide Series"; San Antonio: The Clegg Co., 1938), p. 36.

sufficient to keep pace with Dallas and Houston whereupon San Antonio actually lost its rank as Texas' largest city in 1930.[11] This has been attributed to the fantastic growth of the other cities, but to understand the matter more clearly, it would do well to examine San Antonio's economic background.

San Antonio is located on the San Antonio River 150 miles from the Gulf of Mexico and an equal distance from the Mexican border. The climate is subtropical with temperatures usually ranging from the low fifties to the mid-eighties. The growing season averages over 282 days a year and, since the city lies in the fertile Blackland Prairie, agriculture has always played an important role in San Antonio's growth. Water is supplied by the Edwards limestone aquifer which is the source of the San Antonio River.

Because of good grazing areas, San Antonio's first industry was cattle. The city was used as the starting point for the cattle drives up the Chisholm and other trails. Vast herds raised south and west of the city were rounded-up and driven through San Antonio on their way to the slaughtering centers of the Midwest. San Antonio prospered from the money spent by cowboys and cattle barons, but the coming of the railroad and of fences reduced the benefits of this source. Cattle drives ceased and cattle were shipped by rail to Kansas City and Chicago.

---

[11]U.S., Bureau of Census, Fifteenth Census of the United States: 1930. Population, II, 974.

The area surrounding San Antonio has always been excellent for
raising goats and sheep. Thus, the mohair and wool industries have
prospered. Although most of the nation's wool and mohair has always
come from the San Antonio area, students of economics have been puzzled
by the city's failure to capitalize on the manufacturing of woolen
apparel.

The manufacture of flour was started in 1851 with the establishment of mills by German settlers. Other industries have included
meat packing, dairy farming, cement manufacturing, garment making, and
brewing. One of the oldest industries is the making of food products
like chile con carne which originated in San Antonio. However, in this
century, it has been the oil and gas industries that have provided the
impetus to the San Antonio economy; that is, only if the military is
excluded as an industry.

From its very beginning San Antonio has been a military center.
Founded as a fort and mission, it was a vital post in the maintenance
of Spanish claims on Texas and the Southwest. After Texas joined the
Union, the United States Army set up permanent facilities in the Alamo
and trained volunteers for the Mexican War. The Army's influence and
size grew steadily and in 1875 Fort Sam Houston was started on city-
donated land. Now Headquarters for Fourth Army, Fort Sam Houston has
seen most of America's famed military leaders pass through its gates.
Among these have been the late Generals Douglas MacArthur and "Black-
jack" Pershing and former President Dwight Eisenhower.

The Air Force was born in San Antonio when a biplane purchased from the Wright brothers flew successfully to a height of 115 feet in 1910. Later the country's entire Air Force--six planes--stationed at Fort Sam Houston participated in Pershing's futile chase after Pancho Villa in Mexico. The growth of the Air Force has provided a real boon to the development of San Antonio. Kelly Air Force Base, established in 1917 on the city's southwest corner, has become San Antonio's largest single employer with a payroll for some 20,000 civilians.

There are now seven military installations in the city all of which are vital to its economy. The combined military-civilian payrolls of these installations totalled $303,000,000 in 1964 and accounted for one-fourth of the total personal income of San Antonio.[12] This pattern has been true for the last twenty years or more. However, San Antonio's relationship with the military has not been totally financial, as the many local girls who have married servicemen can testify. The city has even gained the title of "mother-in-law" of the Army and the Air Force.

Whatever a city's geographic or economic characteristics may be, its people give either colorful vitality and uniqueness or drab lifelessness and conformity. San Antonio has always charmed visitors with its cosmopolitan flavor and notably good natured atmosphere. Will Rogers, O. Henry, and Sidney Lanier were enthusiasts of the city and,

---

[12]City of San Antonio, Planning Department, Economic Base Study of San Antonio, Texas, (1964), p. 70.

since they always have been considered among the leading critics of American life, San Antonians treasure their views. These three were unanimous in their views of San Antonio as one of the country's most original and picturesque cities.

The people of San Antonio have merged into a potpourri of culture and quaintness challenged only by that of San Francisco and New Orleans. The three predominant groups which have converged on San Antonio are the Mexican, the German, and the Anglo-Saxon and each has left its mark on the city. Italians, Frenchmen, Swedes, Belgians, Chinese, Poles, and Negroes have influenced the city's make-up just enough to enrich its international seasoning. While the rest of America has had foreign minorities remain foreign until they absorbed the American way of life, San Antonio has received these minorities and adopted their ways of life. Thus, it has been, for instance, Mexican descendants and German immigrants who have influenced San Antonio's characteristics and not vice versa.

The Indian, of course, was the first inhabitant of San Antonio, but most of the tribes were of the Plains group and thus not given to prolonged or massed settlements. When the Spanish arrived they found a small Indian village near the San Pedro Springs, but no large settlement like those of the Navajo in New Mexico and Arizona. Unlike the English and the Americans, the Spanish were not adverse to intermarriage with the Indians; the result was the development of the mestizo ethnic group, well-known to sociologists and anthropologists. This blending of blood produced the Mexican ethnic group which has played one of the major roles in the cultural development of San Antonio.

Spanish influence of the European variety has played a relatively minor role in the city's development. Although San Antonio's first official European settlers were from the Spanish Canary Islands, intermarriage with the Indian, the mestizo, and the American and German settlers coupled with the Mexican Revolution of 1821 diminished most of any influence the Spanish mainland might have provided. This is not to say that Spanish ties were obliterated, but that most of them were transferred to Mexico and the mestizo culture.

San Antonio has always been a gateway to America; only recently has it adopted the title of "gateway to Mexico." America has long been portrayed as a land of opportunity and the natives of Mexico have accepted this. Immigration barriers until recently have been virtually non-existent on the Mexican border. These two factors, along with an above average birth rate among the native born, have greatly increased the number of inhabitants of Mexican origin in San Antonio since 1870 when they comprised only 16 per cent of the city population.[13] This proportion has increased steadily, and in 1940 it was approximated to be 40 per cent of the total population.[14]

---

[13] Ibid., p. 42.

[14] An Economic and Industrial Survey of San Antonio, Texas (Mimeographed bulletin; San Antonio Public Service Co., 1942), p. 176.

Additional factors in the amazing growth of the Mexican population in San Antonio have been: a critical shortage of agricultural labor just after the turn of the century followed by an almost abrupt halt of this need; and the very human impulse of political refugees to flee to a common haven.

Just as San Antonio had been a natural market for Mexican horses and an ideal assembling point for South Texas cattle herds, it became a useful market place for Mexican farm labor. San Antonio became one of the nation's major recruiting centers for farm labor needed in the cotton fields of Texas and the Mississippi Valley and the fruit and vegetable fields of the Midwest. Migratory labor routes radiated out of San Antonio like the spokes of a cartwheel. It is estimated that by 1940 Texas had over 683,000 inhabitants of Mexican extraction, of which 40 per cent were born in Mexico or had parents born there; one-sixth of these lived in San Antonio and many more resided in the surrounding area.[15] Most of them were involved in farm labor and when technical developments diminished their farm usefulness, they gravitated to San Antonio.

The political refugee is a peculiar individual, usually headstrong with a deep sense of loyalty to his country, if not to its governing regime, and a strong desire to return to his native land. In 1910 Francisco Madero, presidential candidate in Mexico, escaped his enemies and established political headquarters in San Antonio. A few

---

[15]Ibid.

months later local supplies of 30-30 rifles and ammunition were brought
out by his revolutionary agents and Madero went on to Mexico and victory.[16] Madero's victory was not permanent, however, and a series of
counter-revolutions sent some 25,000 refugees scurrying to San
Antonio.[17] One of these was Don Leonides Gonzalez who had narrowly
escaped death by a firing squad.

It is doubtful that any other city in this country, except possibly present-day Miami, has experienced the drama of political
intrigue, of plots and counterplots that enveloped San Antonio. Most
of these refugees vowed to return to Mexico, but few did; most of them
longed for their native land, some still do. Since they could not
return home, they did their best to make their refuge as much like
home as possible. They set up newspapers, print shops, bookstores,
food stores, restaurants, and countless other establishments. They
fitted in easily with the Texas-born Mexican and found that they could
live their whole life in the United States without uttering a word of
English. Most refugees are now either deceased or in old age but
their sons and daughters are among the most active people in community
life.

Much of the color and glamor of San Antonio must be attributed
to the Mexican culture. Its contributions can be found in every
aspect of the city's life. The Spanish language is spoken freely and

---

[16]Federal Writers', op. cit., p. 39.

[17]Planning Department, op. cit., p. 126.

extensively, many religious and social customs are still part of city
life, and Spanish surnamed citizens permeate the social, business, and
civic rolls of the community.

The promise of American freedom and opportunity that brought
Mexicans to San Antonio also brought German immigrants. Many were
fugitives from the politics of Germany--intellectuals, craftsmen, and
professionals who preferred to leave the Fatherland in freedom than to
remain in subjugation. They came in large numbers in the 1840's and
for years later. Many settled north of San Antonio in New Braunfels
and in the Hill Country, but most eventually drifted into the city.
By 1870 they became the leading group in the community, comprising 36
per cent of the total population, and dominated the social and business
life.[18]

The importance of the German contribution is well documented
in historical accounts of San Antonio. Probably the most universally
acknowledged contributions are the social customs cultivated by the
German community. Song festivals (Sangarfest) and get-togethers
(Kommers) were held regularly and many still are in the Hill Country.
Exclusive organizations were set up for the benefit of the German community. The famous Casino Association played such an important role
that some say many political and business transactions affecting the
whole city were often made in the Casino Building.

---

[18]Federal Writers', op. cit., p. 21.

The Casino (still standing on the banks of the San Antonio River) was closed to all but those of the German community with the exception of the military. Soldiers, especially officers, were welcomed and were frequent visitors and, though one would hardly expect that any major military decision was made there, it is widely believed that Robert E. Lee spent many pensive hours at the Casino bar before making his fateful decision.

Another popular gathering place for the Germans was Beethoven Hall (still standing in Pereida Street), the scene of many concerts starring some of the most nationally prominent musicians and singers of the day. Many of the political leaders of San Antonio have been, and still are, of German descent and the first bank in San Antonio was set up by a German named Gross. A German language newspaper flourished for several generations and the German-English School provided a solid foundation for the youngsters who were destined to become the city's leading citizens.

The German culture has left a deep imprint on the life of San Antonio. The Teutonic traits of self-discipline and self-reliance, coupled with a tradition of freedom that resulted in their settlement in the area, have had an important effect on the growth of San Antonio. By 1940 there were approximately 40,000 inhabitants of German descent in the city, more than in any other city in Texas and most of the South.[19]

---

[19]Public Service Company, op. cit., p. 21.

The third major ingredient in the cultural potpourri of San Antonio is the American, English, and Irish tradition, to be referred to in this paper as Anglo. The first Anglo settlers in San Antonio were, of course, members of Austin's colonizing party. After them came adventurers, mostly from the Old South; the cowboys and the soldiers then found the city suitable for settlement. The Irish came, with most of them working as teamsters and mechanics. All in all, Anglos who came to San Antonio represented a cross-section of America.

There is not much that can be said of the originality of the Anglos' contribution other than to say that they brought America to San Antonio. If it had not been for them, the city might have become two--a Mexican town and a German town. The American was the catalytic agent in the amalgamation of the Mexican and German cultures into San Antonio's own special brand of Americanism. The American soldier, the cowboy, the traveling salesman, the eastern banker, and others were the ones who linked San Antonio with the rest of the country.

Lest San Antonio's sons and daughters feel resentful, the dramatic and heroic contributions of men like Jim Bowie and Davey Crockett must be mentioned. Americans like these provided Texas and San Antonio with the challenge and the opportunity to achieve their present status.

The Negroes came to San Antonio as slaves. However, they have never provided a major proportion of the population, ranging from about 12 per cent when emancipated during the Civil War to approximately 8

per cent in this century.[20] San Antonio has had fewer Negroes than
any major city in the South. Although they have faced most of the
same problems that confront Negroes everywhere, the degree of discrimination has probably been less in San Antonio than in any city in the
South. Though this does not justify anything short of complete equality, it has served to soothe the conscience of the white citizenry.

San Antonio's people and their heritage have made the city a
cosmopolitan center of America where the cultures of the Western World
join hands. Writers have been led to call San Antonio "city in the
sun," "Spain in Texas," "Mexico in the United States," "Little Rhine-
land," "Cradle of Texas Liberty," "Venice in America," and countless
other colorful and descriptive names. This has made tourism a big
business in San Antonio; visitors flock to the city the year round.
Visitors are seldom disappointed when they see San Antonio, a city
with a flair for the unusual, the new, and the festive combined with
an affectionate attachment to the old and a paradoxical, almost
resentful, suspicion of change.

If San Antonio's cultural environment is a unique combination
of the Old World and the New, its political history provides a similar
combination. A survey of the political past of San Antonio provides a
mixture of events, campaigns, court battles, and elections that portrays
a political environment rivaling Chicago for hooliganism, New York in

---

[20]Ibid., p. 32.

machine control, Wisconsin in progressive reform, and Boston for
Curley-like ethnic politics.

Machine control of the city was freely acknowledged by the
press in 1931 in an article tracing back the "city-county machine"
then in power almost fifty years to its founder Bryan Callaghan. Callaghan, half-Latin, half-Irish, who is said to have conducted the city
like his own private property, served as mayor for twelve years and
county judge for four. His father had been mayor before him; his son
was mayor after him.[21]

In a one-party state dominated by Democrats, San Antonio's
congressional district sent a Republican to Washington for five consecutive terms. It is here that the German influence in politics was
felt. Texans of German descent were notable in their lack of enthusiastic support of the Confederacy in the Civil War and afterwards
leaned heavily to the Republican Party. San Antonio was at that time
in the fourteenth district composed of Bexar County and counties to
the north and east where there was a sizable population of German
extraction, and the result was Republican Harry Wurzbach's successive
terms.

Reform politics appeared in San Antonio in the early 1930's
when a group of bipartisan citizens decided to challenge the machine
in a bond election. After a close election the machine's victory was
successfully challenged in court and its hold temporarily loosened.

---

[21] San Antonio Light, July 13, 1931.

However, control of city and county government remained for the most part in the hands of the remnants of the Callaghan machine until the late 1940's.

Throughout the city's history, citizens of Mexican ancestry[22] have played a major, though not always effective, role in politics. One of Callaghan's closest associates was county Tax Collector Joe Cassiano, for whom a city park is now named. An attempt to bar Latin Americans from voting in Austin, Texas, led a San Antonio newspaper to write that this "would have disfranchised at least 30 per cent of San Antonio's voting population." The paper added that voters of Mexican ancestry "have voted since time immemorial in Bexar County."[23] A grand jury investigation in 1930 revealed that voting in Bexar County was not limited to American citizens, as many aliens were casting ballots without regard for the statutory provisions requiring citizenship as a voting prerequisite.

During the Prohibition Era the county was known as the "Free State of Bexar" because not one conviction for violation of prohibition laws was ever obtained.[24] At the beginning of World War II San Antonio was known as the "most wide open city in the United States" and had an infamous red light district marked by disease, brawls, shakedowns, and

---

[22]To avoid confusion, United States residents of Mexican ancestry hereafter will be referred to as Latin Americans.

[23]San Antonio News, July 26, 1934.

[24]The Washington Post, October 14, 1934.

political payoffs. The mayor in 1937 reportedly sought a pardon during a presidential audience for the alleged head of the city's lottery business who had been convicted of income tax evasion.[25]

Politicians were known to have engaged in courtroom fisticuffs and attempted knifings. A noted gambler seriously wounded a rival with a shotgun, was freed on a technicality, and shortly thereafter attracted sizable votes in unsuccessful campaigns for district attorney, police commissioner, and state senator. (This man, V. E. "Red" Berry, now a retired gambler, is currently serving a third consecutive term in the Texas House of Representatives.) Maury Maverick, a controversial and outspoken New Deal congressman, was defeated in a hysterical red-baiting campaign. Later Maverick was elected mayor, but was defeated after he upheld the rental of the city's auditorium to a few local communists and a huge crowd outside rioted in protest.

Yet, for all its controversy and recklessness, the city usually appeared quiet, restful, and sparkling to the casual visitor. The war had brought about many changes to San Antonio, mainly through the huge military concentration that engulfed the city. But no matter how quaint or unique the city appeared to the visitor, many of its citizens had become aware of a hidden city of disease, poverty, illiteracy, and filth.

During the first thirty years of the twentieth century San Antonio quadrupled its size to almost a quarter of a million

---

[25]Owen P. White, "Machine Made," Colliers, September 18, 1937.

inhabitants. The Latin American population took a fantastic jump of 840 per cent and rose from 25 per cent of the population to 35 per cent. In 1930 Latin Americans totalled approximately 82,373, a number almost 30,000 higher than San Antonio's total population in 1900.[26]

The city was not prepared for such an abrupt change in its make-up. During the years that San Antonio was sprouting and soldiers and tourists were marvelling at the quaintness of the Mexican market place, the "Chile Queens," and the strolling troubadours, it was becoming more and more burdened with a problem few cities are asked to carry. Relatively segregated on the west side of town, most Latin Americans were wallowing in disease, poverty, filth, and illiteracy which was unparalleled in the worst slums of the East or the deep South. The nationally-noted correspondent, Heywood Broun, called San Antonio's slums "the worst in America."[27]

Yet, ironically, the oil, gas, and cattle industries were swelling the bank accounts of the city's leading citizens during this period. One of the leading contributors to the national Democratic campaign fund in 1932 was a San Antonio resident. He directed a multi-million dollar cattle, oil, and related business that had national and even international impacts. And there were many more like him. Yet in most cases the city's only contact with Latin Americans was when

---

[26]U.S., Bureau of Census, Fifteenth Census, loc. cit.

[27]Green Peyton, San Antonio, City in the Sun (New York: Whittlesey House, 1946), p. 120.

they did its labor. This attitude did not go unnoticed to a sociolo-
gist who observed: "What strikes one forcibly who has looked into
their [Latin Americans] life in San Antonio is the utter indifference
of the community to their presence; it is an indifference which is pal-
pable, almost blatant."[28]

However, San Antonio was not interested in the criticisms of
sociologists as witnessed by the exaggerated writing of one:

> San Antonio . . . is run by Texans, cattlemen with a history
> of individualism that renders insipid the rugged individualism of
> your northern industrialist. Outside advice in once independent
> Texas, and in San Antonio, which is rather super-Texas, is a thing
> that is definitely nongrata.[29]

Of course, the depression deepened the quandry of Latin Americans, but this made little difference to the rest of the city which
had begun to feel the effects of the economic crisis. The city's
growth came to an almost complete halt as the rate diminished to a
meagre 10 per cent from 1930 to 1940.[30] However, the city was shocked
into reality when the discovery was made that Latin Americans had
absorbed all the increase in population in the ten-year period from
1930 to 1940. The city had grown by only 22,000 and the Latin American population increased 21,000.[31] The city's reaction to this

---

[28]Max Handman, "San Antonio, the Old Capital City of Mexican
Life and Influence," The Survey, LXVI (May, 1931), 164.

[29]Kathryn Close, "Sick Men Can't Fight," Survey Graphic,
reprint (March, 1943), p. 3.

[30]U.S., Bureau of Census, Sixteenth Census of the United
States: 1940. Population, II, 971.

[31]Public Service Company, op. cit., p. 176.

discovery can be best described in the words of an official "fact finding committee" of civic leaders which concluded that "in San Antonio and its suburbs the Latin American population is the most serious problem."[32]

The "problem" had finally been discovered and the committee's facts found that it was not poverty or unemployment, disease or illiteracy, but the "Latin American population." The problem now pinpointed, the solution was simple--remove it. How?: "It is believed that consideration should be given to the redistribution of population, and that some of these families should voluntarily return to the small towns and farms from which they have come and that other families should be repatriated."[33]

The committee's answer to the problem was not an isolated one, since two years later a survey undertaken to find methods of attracting industry to the city concluded:

> Replacement of 35 per cent of the Latin Americans by an equivalent number of economically independent families would transform San Antonio, socially, politically, economically, and in health. It would increase its tourist and convention business. It would help attract industry. It would raise the whole standard of living.[34]

---

[32]American Public Welfare Association, Public Welfare Survey of San Antonio, Texas (Chicago: American Public Welfare Association, 1940), Appendix A.

[33]Ibid.

[34]Public Service Company, op. cit., 123.

These proposed solutions led qualified observers to write: "Americans are notoriously inept and unimaginative in their relations with foreign groups and San Antonians are no exception."[35]

A glance at some figures confirms the seriousness of the problem that so exasperated San Antonio's leadership. A survey of housing conditions in 1939 revealed that, of 75,677 families in the metropolitan area, 39,515 families, or 53 per cent, lived in substandard housing. Of these families, 18,124 were Latin American, 68 per cent of which had incomes of less than $550 per year. Much of the housing consisted of "corrals" which were one-story tenement quarters of a series of cubicles, each of which served as living quarters for a whole family. They usually had communal open surface privies that contributed to fly breeding and spread communicable disease and child intestinal disorders.[36]

Disease was rampant as diarrhea and tuberculosis teamed up as the city's number one killers of inhabitants from birth to the age of thirty-nine. In 1939 the infant death rate among Latin Americans was twice the national average. Latin American infants had little chance for survival as they represented 70 per cent of infant deaths from

[35]American Public Welfare Association, op. cit., 24.

[36]City of San Antonio Housing Authority, San Antonio Housing Survey, 1939 (San Antonio: San Antonio Housing Authority, 1940), pp. 1-46.

1941 to 1945. And one in twenty Latin Americans was a victim of tuberculosis in 1945.[37]

The child who happened to survive had poor odds of obtaining
an education. One qualified observer estimated that of every 200 Latin
American children who entered school, only half finished the first
grade, 45 completed the eighth, 36 entered high school, only 22 graduated, and just 1 entered college. Approximately 3,000 children of
Mexican descent never even entered school and almost all of the estimated 550 paper and shoeshine boys on the streets during school hours
were Latin Americans.[38]

Jobs and good wages were hard to come by as 80 per cent of all
placements by the Texas Employment Service were for 30 days or less,
with pay for more than half of those placed averaging only $6 per week.
In eight cities of comparable size, San Antonio ranked eighth in average weekly income with $20.18 while first place Oakland, California,
averaged $26.94.[39] Yet in San Antonio, even taking into account the
Chamber of Commerce claim that living costs in this city were less
than elsewhere, it was estimated that an average family had to earn
$1,400 annually for minimum health and efficiency in 1940.[40] Indeed,

---

[37]City of San Antonio, Department of Health, City Health
Department, 1946-47, March, 1947, pp. 12-16.

[38]American Public Welfare Association, op. cit., pp. 89-90.

[39]Ibid.

[40]Public Service Company, op. cit., p. 115.

not earning enough money

many Latin Americans earned less than $550 and 75 per cent earned less than $950 annually.[41]

World War II was an economic blessing immediately for San Antonio and eventually for the city's Latin Americans. The city was engulfed in a massive military build-up that hired the unemployed and gave many of them skills; it poured millions into the local economy in construction and purchasing; and military-civilian payrolls swelled the city's pocketbooks. The city once again began to grow; in fact, during the period between 1940 and 1950, San Antonio grew at a rate of over 60 per cent as the population jumped to over 500,000 in the metropolitan area.[42]

After the war there was substantial improvement in the economic fortunes of the city. However, Latin Americans still struggled for survival. Their children still had the highest death rate in the city and accounted for 64 per cent of infant deaths in 1946. The city had the highest death rate for cities over 100,000 population.[43] Most, if not all, of the problems that faced Latin Americans before the war still persisted. However, one change did occur. That was in the Latin-American veterans. Home from the battle fronts of Europe, Africa, and the Pacific they were no longer resigned to live in

---

[41]Housing Authority, op. cit., p. 12.

[42]U.S., Bureau of Census, Seventeenth Census of the United States: 1950. Population, II, 43-204.

[43]Health Department, op. cit., pp. 7-11.

substandard housing, and to work at jobs for cheap wages, and to endure sickness as a course of life.

The real story of the contributions of the "GI Bill of Rights" has yet to be written, but it was the Emancipation Proclamation of San Antonio's Latin Americans. They knew that their success hinged on education and the GI Bill provided it for them. Many finished high school, learned trades, and, in many instances, completed college and gained professional status. The war had given them a whole new perspective on the world and on life. It was in this new frame of reference that they undertook to gain educations. They knew that they had contributed to American success in the war and now they were ready to reap the benefits.

As Latin Americans became more educated, they became more politically aware. They began to demand more in return for their votes in elections as they learned the power of political unity. They organized in groups dedicated to bettering the conditions of la raza (the race) like the GI Forum and strengthened similar organizations that already existed like the League of United Latin American Citizens (LULAC). They protested the segregation of their children in public schools and successfully asked the courts to prohibit the policy. They felt that they were illegally being classified as a separate race, when they were actually Caucasians, and the courts agreed.[44] They took their case to the courts when restrictions were placed in

[44] Hernandez v. Texas, 347 U.S. 475 (1954).

contracts preventing them from buying property outside slums and the court removed the restrictions.[45] (But they knew that the courts could only give them protection within a legal framework and it was political officeholders who held the key to their success or failure.)

Finally, in 1948 Latin Americans joined forces with Negroes to astound the city, the state, and the nation in a political coup that exhibited political sagacity believed unknown to the participants. Don Politico, an anonymous reporter for a San Antonio newspaper, called it a "potent combination of San Antonio minorities," that elected attorney Gus Garcia to the San Antonio Independent School District Board and Negro businessman G. J. Sutton as a Junior College Trustee.[46]

Don Politico observed that "for the first time the West Side stuck together on a Latin candidate. Hitherto it had been possible to split it into two factions." He added that "now citizens' groups, even from the West Side, will be heard. . . ."[47]

Although a major breakthrough had been achieved, problems continued to plague Latin Americans and consequently the city also. It was found that in 1950 the areas of the city that contained over 90 per cent Latin-American population provided most of the cases for state aid to dependent children, had the highest concentration of delinquency, and provided the most deaths from tuberculosis and infant diarrhea.

---

[45]Clifton v. Puente, 218 SW 2d 272 (1948) Texas Court of Appeals.

[46]San Antonio Light, April 4, 1948.

[47]Ibid.

The area was conclusively the least socio-economically advantaged in San Antonio.[48]

With the minor exception of a justice of the peace and a constable, there was no major Latin-American officeholder in San Antonio and the "potent combination of minorities" had failed to come up with further coups. There appeared to be no one who could reap the political harvest of a minority combination and also convince enough Anglos to support him. In retrospect the potential for success seemed certain, but, at the time, there appeared no one who believed it possible.

---

[48]Recreation: An Essential Community Service (Mimeographed survey; Community Welfare Council, San Antonio, Texas, 1954), pp. 7-14.

CHAPTER II

AN INTRODUCTION TO THE MAN

The exciting and colorful cosmopolitan flavor that is unique
to San Antonio has helped to develop, in Henry B. Gonzalez, a politician who mirrors the city's historical tradition and, at the same time,
reflects its potential for the future. Of course, Gonzalez successfully united the "potent combination" referred to in the preceding
chapter[1] with enough Anglo support to gain a series of unprecedented
city-wide election victories and to become one of San Antonio's most
successful politicians. Gonzalez' success is partially explained by
his early social and intellectual development. Hence, for the purpose
of this study, it is necessary that his pre-political life be examined
in light of his later achievements.

Henry B. Gonzalez is a first generation American of Mexican
ancestry. His parents fled Mexico during the revolutionary uprisings
of 1910 and found refuge in San Antonio in 1911. His father, Leonides
Gonzalez Cigarroa, and his mother, Genoveva Barbosa Prince de Gonzalez,
had no intention of remaining in San Antonio; they planned to stay only
until it was safe to return to their home in Mapimi, Durango. In this
atmosphere of anticipation of returning to Mexico, three boys and a girl

---

[1]
Above, p. 28.

were born to Leonides and Genoveva; it was in this same atmosphere
that the six children, including the fourth child, Enrique (Henry), were
raised. The two oldest children, Leonides and Carlos were born in Mexico.

In Mexico, Leonides operated silver mines in the metal-rich
area around the town of Mapimi in the State of Durango. He was also
Mayor of Mapimi. The whole area was extremely productive and provided
a vital financial service to the central government in Mexico City.
Shortly after Francisco Madero's successful revolution in 1910, a band
of local insurgents, who later joined with Pancho Villa, assumed control, demanded huge monetary tributes, and arrested the mayor who was
a symbol of the hated government of Porfirio Diaz.

Leonides was taken before a firing squad, but a woman general, who
previously had been befriended by the mayor, averted the execution when
a merchant's wife reminded her of the mayor's good deed. An agreement
for payment of tribute--almost all of the Gonzalez' possessions--was
made, along with an understanding that Gonzalez would leave the country.
With this episode behind them, the Gonzalez couple fled to San Antonio.

By this time, Mexico was in bitter turmoil and confusion. The
trip to the American border was a difficult and dangerous one. At one
stop Leonides and his wife were trapped in the cross fire of rival
revolutionary groups. Fortunately, they escaped unharmed and arrived
in San Antonio in February, 1911, after a brief stay in Laredo.[2]

---

[2] Interview with Leonides Gonzalez, June 4, 1964.

Now strangers in a foreign country, the Gonzalezes ached to return to the land their ancestors had colonized. Leonides was a descendant of the original Spanish colonizers of Durango in 1534. His wife, Genoveva, was the great-granddaughter of Cosmo Prince, a Scotch-Irish Presbyterian who, in the mid-1850's, went to Mexico from Pennsylvania and married the daughter of a Spanish merchant in Saltillo. (On several occasions, this Irish background prompted Henry Gonzalez to amusingly tease John F. Kennedy by quipping: "We Irish have to stick together.")[3]

In 1913 Leonides became managing editor of La Prensa, a new Spanish-language daily. The newspaper became the voice of Mexican intellectuals and politicians who, at that time, were conspicuous by their great numbers in San Antonio. Although its policy changed considerably later, during its first years the newspaper devoted its pages almost exclusively to political, cultural, and social developments in Mexico.

The Gonzalez home at 217 Upson Street, located a short distance northwest of the downtown area, proved to be a haven for intellectual, religious, and political refugees from Mexico, and they often participated in evening discussions which lasted into the early hours of morning. Topics included politics, religion, literature, art, music, and life in general. Henry, who was born May 3, 1916, remembers

---

[3]Interview with Henry B. Gonzalez, May 12, 1964.

that Jose Vasconcelos, the Mexican historian, often visited the house and participated in the discussions.

The tightly-knit, interdependent Gonzalez family was modeled after the families of the patriarchal society of Mexico. The father, Leonides, was the unchallenged head of the household and ruled with a stern hand, demanding complete obedience. Genoveva, the mother, was a warm, understanding, exceedingly astute woman, who dampened Leonides' firmness and implanted a keen knowledge of human behavior in her children through the use of proverbs, epigrams, and Mexican folklore.

Upson Street, where the house was located, was in a middle-class neighborhood. The area around the Gonzalez home provided one of the "best possible environments for anyone to grow up in," with Anglo, German, and Latin-American--both Mexican-born and American-born--families living together in relative harmony.[4] Families in the neighborhood provided a microcosm of San Antonio, ranging from the financially independent to the very poor and from the highly cultured to the unrefined. One block away was the Riverside Gang, whose members often clashed with young Henry Gonzalez.

The Gonzalez children were of above average intelligence and exceptionally talented. For instance, Carlos had an exceptional aptitude for mathematics and even lectured classes while still an undergraduate at Rice Institute. Luz, the only girl, was a talented musician, who, until her marriage, was expected to soar to great heights as a

---

[4]Ibid.

concert pianist. Melchor was a natural athlete who excelled at Jefferson High School and expected a football scholarship to Texas A. & M. College until he learned that "Mexicans" were not awarded scholarships. Leonides, Jr., the eldest, became a mining engineer, and Joaquin breezed through medical school. Henry was always an avid reader; he studied pre-engineering at San Antonio College and obtained a law degree at St. Mary's University.

The home offered ample opportunity for cultural and musical development (most of the family can still play piano). Each of the children seemed to have "an inborn curiosity which led to good reading habits." However, Henry was the primary beneficiary of his father's extensive library. He acquired an early fondness for Spanish literature. His brother, Joaquin, remembers, "Papa would bring home books obtained through La Prensa's library and Henry would be the one to read them."[5] The books were all in Spanish and Henry was the only child who cultivated a Spanish reading habit.

In 1958, during Henry Gonzalez' campaign for governor, Ronnie Dugger, a critical student of Texas politics and editor of the Texas Observer, described Gonzalez' early reading habits:

> At eight Henry began becoming "intimately acquainted with the San Antonio public library." His first devotion was to a series of Western novels by an author he has forgotten. In time he developed his tastes in history, biography, law and philosophy. He used to copy out Matthew Arnold's essays word for word. He found, at home, a first edition of Ortega y Gasset's Revolt of the Masses, he read through Thier's history of the French Revolution

---

5
 Interview with Dr. Joaquin Gonzalez, February 18, 1965.

in Spanish; LeBon's treatise on atoms and fission at 15; at 16,
Descartes's Essay on Method; all of Thomas Carlyle, including his
history of the French Revolution; Leplace, LeComte, Jeremy Bentham,
Locke, Hobbes, "especially John Stuart Mill--I really like him"'
Sarmiento Argentinan, Baltazar Gracian, Spanish names; St. John of
the Cross, Fray Luis de Granada, Spanish mystics, "tremendous
writers!"; Salvador Madariaga, Calderon; Spanish dramatist Unamuno,
Pio Baroja, Santayana.[6]

Young Henry's intellectual curiosity and extensive reading allowed
him to partake in stimulating conversations with his father--a privilege
his siblings seldom shared. Joaquin recalls: "There seemed to be
more communication between Papa and Henry than between Papa and the
rest of us."[7]   In addition, Henry sometimes joined the political discussions between his father and his uncle, Dr. Joaquin Gonzalez Cigarroa.
But this intellectual dialogue with his father did not prevent Henry
from challenging parental authority. He possessed a rebellious nature
which often led to open conflicts with his father.

As a young boy Gonzalez was aggressive in his contacts with
playmates. Often friends would pit him against other boys and goad
them to fight. Gonzalez usually won, but when he lost he did not rest
until he was able to reverse the verdict. On noting the mischief his
own children create, he recalled the group of boys he organized to
systematically raid a neighborhood grocer's cookie barrel. One of
them would divert the grocer's attention and the others would sneak in
and grab handfuls of cookies. The practice was ended, however, when

---

6
    Ronnie Dugger, "Henry Gonzalez, His Life and Times," The
Texas Observer, June 13, 1958.

7
    Dr. Gonzalez interview, op. cit.

two of the boys were caught in an attempt to conduct their own raid.
Gonzalez remembers that, although he was always a prime suspect, he
was never caught red-handed.[8]

p answer word

But other than engaging in the multitude of pranks that fill
the childhood of any aggressive boy, Gonzalez did not present his parents with major disciplinary problems. This, however, was not beyond
the realm of possibility, since some of the neighborhood boys were
members of the Riverside Gang and eventually were sent to prison. On
the other hand, Gonzalez' appetite for books led him to spend hours
reading and thus kept him close to the house or in the public library.

The wages of a newspaperman provided the Gonzalez family with
an adequate, though far from comfortable, living. For awhile, Leonides'
brother and his family lived with them. Leonides was the only one
employed and this caused a financial strain on both families. Consequently, Henry was prompted to find part-time work. His first job was
in the drug store of a retired German sea captain, Ernst Von Helms.
Von Helms was a strict disciplinarian who regularly frightened away
delivery boys with his demanding orders given half in German and half
in broken English. But ten-year-old "Enrico," as Von Helms called him,
was not easily frightened, and he stayed more than a year, graduating
to part-time clerk and soda jerk.

Von Helms taught "Enrico" to mop, to speak a little German, to
be self-reliant and resourceful. Von Helms was extremely interested in

---

[8]Interview with Henry B. Gonzalez, December 29, 1964.

world politics and engaged his customers in long discussions. Whenever
he could not recall a historical date or a particular name or fact,
Von Helms would turn to his young employee for the answer with the
words: "Enrico knows." (This ability to retain historical data has
proved invaluable to Gonzalez in his political career.) Von Helms's
interest in world politics revolved around the thought of Germany's
rightful place at the head of all nations. Gonzalez recalls that the
old sea captain was involved in some peculiar dealings which, in the
light of developments since then, may have dealt with secret communica-
tions with Germany. However, Gonzalez discounts the question of
espionage and attributes it more to ardent love of Fatherland.[9]

Young Gonzalez presupposed everyone was filled with an ardent
love and devotion of one's native country. Gonzalez' family loved
Mexico and Von Helms was devoted to Germany. He saw nothing unusual in
this until a teacher corrected him when he told her he was a "Mexican."
She convinced him that, since he was born in the United States, he was
an American, not a Mexican. This seemed logical to Gonzalez until he
brought the matter up at home and "Nana" (name given to a housekeeper-
governess in the Mexican culture) ridiculed him by saying, "I guess if
a cat is born in an oven, that makes him a loaf of bread."[10] This
jolted his senses and carved a deep impression on his mind. The

---

[9] Interview with Henry B. Gonzalez, April 7, 1964.
[10] Ibid.

ambivalent atmosphere that the family was living in was rudely brought to his attention. Was he American or Mexican?

Although he was an avid reader, even before beginning his formal education, Gonzalez' first school year was difficult. He knew no English ("I couldn't even say mama") and consequently he remained in low first for a full year.[11] However, once he learned English, he advanced quickly and even skipped a grade.

He was athletically inclined and enjoyed playing sandlot football, baseball, and basketball. He also exercised in the back yard and sparred with his cousins and friends. Usually he excelled in events that required an individual effort, such as boxing; or, when on an athletic team, he played the key position such as pitcher. From the very first, Gonzalez was an individualist, somewhat of a "lone wolf."[12]

Gonzalez attended Mark Twain Junior High and then Main Avenue High School. When Jefferson High opened, he transferred to the new school and was graduated in 1935. Then he attended San Antonio Junior College, specializing in pre-engineering courses. The faculty at the junior college recognized his potential when he won an intramural vocabulary contest and this prompted him to continue his education at The University of Texas. Gonzalez' college transcript indicates that he was an average student academically with a marked interest and

---

[11]Ibid.

[12]Dr. Gonzalez interview, op. cit.

aptitude in the social sciences. In history and government his grades were A's and B's, but in mathematics and the physical sciences they were C's.[13]

His oratorical ability did not come easily for two reasons. First, he had labored diligently to overcome a heavy Mexican accent by reading aloud with marbles in his mouth in the manner of Demosthenes, and by persuading a friend to correct his speech as he read aloud from Robert Louis Stevenson's books. He also remembers his sister and brothers creeping up to catch him orating before a mirror.[14] Secondly, he was forced to overcome shyness that had suddenly come upon him at the age of sixteen. Although he had been aggressive and extroverted in childhood, his teens were marked by a change to a reticent, almost inhibited adolescent.[15]

His experience at The University of Texas was chaotic and he stayed only a year. It was in the latter part of the depression and money was scarce. Gonzalez and his brother, Joaquin, shared a room in a boarding house run by two spinster sisters. The brothers worked for their board, one meal a day, by cleaning rooms. Gonzalez also worked twenty hours a week for five dollars with the Austin Exterminating Company. At times he managed to find odd jobs to supplement his income, such as a translating job in a district court insurance case where he so impressed the judge that his pay was doubled.

---

[13]Transcript of grades of Henry B. Gonzalez.

[14]Dugger, op. cit.

[15]Dr. Gonzalez interview, op. cit.

The Gonzalez brothers spent a cold and hungry winter at the University. They could not afford a heater and, consequently, learned of the warmth of newspaper blankets. One meal each per day was not enough for energetic students and the Gonzalez boys often felt the pangs of hungry stomachs. Gonzalez recalls that one of the other tenants received a food package from home every week, which he put aside for snacks. Since he had access to the boy's room for cleaning, Gonzalez often helped himself to the tacos and sandwiches in the package. He also recalls causing an uproar when he ate one too many bananas which were locked in the refrigerator he had been assigned to clean.[16]

Austin was not an easy town for Latin Americans. Discrimination was subtle in some areas, open in others. Students of Mexican descent could not get jobs near the University and had to go out quite a distance to find work. When they had enough money to buy a meal, Latin Americans were not free to choose the cafe of their choice. They were often called "greasers" or "spics." Although the same attitude was found in San Antonio, Gonzalez had the security of his family and friends to help him cope with it. Austin was a strange, unfamiliar city which never gave any indication of wanting to accept Gonzalez.

Joaquin was able to join the Texas part of the National Youth Administration administered by Lyndon Johnson, but a one-member-per-family stipulation kept Henry from joining. Then Gonzalez lost his

---

[16]Interview with Henry B. Gonzalez, December 31, 1964.

jobs and developed anemia, so he decided to return home. The cold, hunger, and overall adversity experienced in Austin left harsh memories in Gonzalez' mind--memories that would haunt him in later years [17]

Back in San Antonio, Gonzalez enrolled in St. Mary's University School of Law. He worked his way through with a $30 a month job in the law library. Dean Henry B. Diehlmann helped him obtain a part-time job with the city as a clerk in the Ehrenborg Tax Resurvey during his senior year. He was unable to pay his tuition before graduation in 1940 and received a blank paper instead of a diploma. He didn't receive his diploma until several months later when he finally managed to pay the tuition bill by working for Louie's Cut-Rate Drugs for $12 weekly and at a package store as manager for $14 weekly.[18]

Gonzalez says he never had a date until 1938 when he was twenty-two and was "'backward,' socially speaking."[19] This backwardness, however, did not keep him from unexpectedly returning from a vacation in Mexico to be with Bertha Cuellar. Apparently his parents were anxious that he finish law school before marriage and convinced him to take a two week summer vacation in Mexico at a relative's ranch. The two weeks were stretched into a month before Gonzalez rebelled, rode horseback to a railroad station, and "hopped" a train for San Antonio. He surprised everyone with his presence at Bertha's home.

---

[17]Ibid.

[18]Paul Thompson, "Top of the News," San Antonio Evening News, April 29, 1953.

[19]Dugger, op. cit.

Bertha's family had moved to San Antonio from nearby Flores-
ville and her mother and Gonzalez' mother became good friends. It was
through their families that Bertha and Gonzalez met. Bertha, four
years younger than Gonzalez, remembers that at dances he would ask her
for a set, then engage her in conversation about books he had read so
that they usually ended up "just talking" at one end of the dance
floor. She says that books were the main thing they had in common and
recalls that "we were both avid readers."[20] They were married in 1940
before Gonzalez graduated from law school and now have eight children.

In his political campaigns, the question of Gonzalez' bar
examination has arisen several times. Gonzalez did go to Austin to
take the examination, but he never completed it. He was forced to
leave in the middle of the test because a boil closed his left eye and
became so irritating that he could not continue. Although he prepared
for it at later times, he never again took the bar examination and,
consequently, has never practiced law.

Shortly after Pearl Harbor he was called into government service as a civilian cable and radio censor under military and naval
intelligence. He served two years and then tried unsuccessfully to
join the Federal Bureau of Investigation. In 1943 he accepted a position as assitant juvenile probation officer with the assurance that
there were "no politics mixed in the deal."[21]

---

[20]Interview with Mrs. Henry B. Gonzalez, February 18, 1965.

[21]Ted Deming, Jr., in unmarked clipping in Gonzalez' pre-
political scrapbook.

Devotion to duty, resourcefulness, and hard work quickly earned
Gonzalez a promotion to first assistant. He gave each case individual
attention and insisted on developing a policy of home visits. He said,
"You have to go to 'em. . . . Lord Jesus Christ went among the sinners.
He didn't sit on a swivel chair doing case work."[22]

He worked eighteen-to-twenty-hour days with juveniles and
addressed civic groups about the operations of the juvenile office. He
was quick to point out injustices in the treatment of juveniles or in
the operations of the office, and courthouse reporters began to quote
him extensively.

In 1946 he became the first Latin American and the youngest
chief juvenile probation officer in San Antonio's history. In this
position, Gonzalez, in a newspaper interview, exhibited the philosophy
that underlies the operations of his political offices. He commented
that he favored closer cooperation between law enforcement agencies,
development of inservice training projects for case workers, individual case study as opposed to mass disposition, and improvement of
the educational aspects of crime prevention.[23]

As juvenile probation officer Gonzalez learned that individuals
in positions of public trust, who have definite areas of responsibility, often are aware of facts and situations not commonly known. He
felt that it was his duty to produce factual information concerning

---

[22]Dugger, op. cit.

[23]San Antonio Light, July 7, 1946.

treatment of juveniles in Bexar County. For this purpose he worked
with sociology students from St. Mary's University and Trinity University in special studies and surveys of juvenile problems. One of these
studies indicated that 10,000 juveniles had been incarcerated in city
jail in a three-year period, often for no valid reason. After the
results of the study were revealed, public opinion was organized
against such a practice and two years later the system of incarcerat-
ing juveniles was changed.

Gonzalez often raised his voice when he objected to police or
court treatment of juveniles. When Juvenile Judge Charles Anderson
asked him to maintain segregated offices by isolating a voluntary
Negro caseworker on the East Side, Gonzalez refused and allowed her to
office with the rest of the staff downtown. This marked the beginning
of an unpleasant relationship with Judge Anderson which eventually
resulted in Gonzalez' resignation.

He complained when Anderson did not allow him to select his
own assistants. He said Anderson sent him one sixty-seven-year-old
man "who couldn't walk up the stairs and who believed boys in trouble
were punks who ought to go to jail."[24] Gonzalez resigned over this
issue and said: "If I do not have the right to hire and fire I am not
interested in the position. . . ." The judges of the criminal district
courts who had jurisdiction over the juvenile office withheld his

---

[24]Ibid.

resignation and agreed to "tell the county judge to let Gonzalez run the juvenile office."[25]

However, no reconciliation was made and Gonzalez' resignation was eventually accepted. In over three years in the juvenile office, Gonzalez visited more than 10,000 homes. When he resigned, only six San Antonio youths were in Gatesville, the state boys' correctional institution. This was a considerable number less than in years before or after his tenure. The rate of juvenile delinquency was down 36 per cent when he left. His record prompted the San Antonio Council of Parents and Teachers to officially express regret over his resignation and praise him as "an officer who took very seriously the needs and problems of girls and boys."[26]

Working in the juvenile office had given Gonzalez "his first real test of life" as he learned that "people will be themselves and not what you want them to be." He learned to be prepared for the unexpected as one crisis would arise, be solved, and another would follow without warning. He found it best to "temper" crises and put them in proper perspective. He learned that people and events cannot be controlled, yet public officials are expected to cope with each unexpected development and all its ramifications. For this reason he has expressed concern for the man who goes to Congress "cold" and unprepared.[27]

---

[25]Unmarked newspaper clipping in Gonzalez' scrapbook.

[26]San Antonio Evening News, November 28, 1946.

[27]Interview with Henry B. Gonzales, February 21, 1965.

The controversy with Judge Anderson left Gonzalez with an unpleasant taste for politicians inasmuch as he was convinced that the issue was politically inspired. Yet, his main concern was working with juveniles as he noted in a newspaper interview: "Working with boys is my life's work. One way or another, I'm going to see that they get an even break--politicians or no politicians."[28] Thus, in 1946 at the age of thirty he displayed no political ambitions; his main concerns were boys and providing for his family.

However, in the years that followed, Gonzalez' political interests were developing rapidly. He participated in the activities of numerous Latin-American improvement organizations. He became aware of the influence officeholders had on policies affecting the poor, the uneducated, and the sick. The shyness that carried him through his teens and early twenties was overcome while working in the juvenile office; and he had developed a talent for making statements that made good newspaper copy. In essence, the four-year period between his resignation from the juvenile office in 1946 and his first election bid in 1950 was a time of political fermentation for Gonzalez.

After resigning as chief probation officer, his first job was as executive-secretary of the Junior Deputies of America. The organization was financed by the Kiwanis Club and was organized to work with delinquents. When operational funds were exhausted and Gonzalez was

---

[28]Deming, op. cit.

released, sixty-six Junior Deputies signed a petition threatening resignation if he were not reinstated.)

hired by Papa

In 1947 a group of Latin-American businessmen formed the Pan American Progressive Association (PAPA) and hired Gonzalez as executive-secretary. He was an activist in this position and assisted people who were in need of better living conditions. For example, he helped get water piped into one of the West Side slum sections. As executive-secretary for PAPA, he was responsible for one of the major break-throughs for Latin Americans against discrimination. This occurred when he initiated the organization's interest in the Puente case, which involved the right of Latin Americans to buy property in restricted areas.

He said that he became interested in the Puente case when he read of the amicus curie brief filed by the Solicitor General in the Shelley v. Kraemer restrictive covenant case. He was convinced that Puente had a legal right to purchase a home despite a restrictive covenant against such a purchase and felt that PAPA should help the veteran. While the case was being tried, the Supreme Court ruled against restrictive covenants in the Shelley case and Judge S. G. Tayloe of the Forty-Fifth District Court (Bexar County) ruled in Puente's behalf following the Supreme Court's lead.[29]

Although the Puente victory was a personal triumph for Gonzalez, his activities caused friction with PAPA members and he resigned.

---

[29] Interview with Henry B. Gonzalez, February 26, 1965.

Gonzalez himself has said that he was moved to resign when he found that some of the organization's board members "didn't know what it was all about."[30] Fermentation was now in process.

In 1948 he decided he "could earn $300 a month on my own hook and not take all that baloney," and opened an office in the Houston Building.[31] There he operated a Spanish-English translating service; he also wrote for bicultural publications. He became Educational Director for the International Ladies Garment Workers Union and taught the members English and citizenship. He also taught mathematics at Sidney Lanier High School in the Veterans' Training Program. Although he did not realize it at the time, he was developing his political acumen with each of these positions.

He was active in religious and civic affairs, usually in a position of leadership. His interest in the well-being of boys led him to serve six years as scoutmaster of the Boy Scout troop at San Fernando Cathedral, and, at one time, he seriously considered following a career in professional scouting. He manifested his religious and civic interests by serving as President of the San Fernando Holy Name Society and as first President of the Bishops' Committee for the Spanish Speaking.

Gonzalez' name was by now well-known to the people of San Antonio. He published the English & Spanish Review, a magazine devoted

---

[30]Ibid.

[31]Dugger, op. cit.

to the literary and social issues of interest to bicultural San Antonians, in 1949. The magazine enjoyed momentary distinction when George Santayana responded favorably to an article devoted to an analysis of his philosophy. However, it proved unprofitable and only five issues were published. Gonzalez accepted speaking engagements to discuss various topics including the problems of migrant workers. He was a popular master of ceremonies at events sponsored by the numerous Latin-American social clubs. Newspaper articles referred to him as a "San Antonio civic leader."[32]

Probably the best illustration of his political philosophy before entering active politics appeared in an article in which he wrote:

> Thomas Jefferson never hesitated to challenge ancient tyrannies or old customs if they stood in the way of the common man's liberties and dignity. He proved that when Americans look forward boldly, and honestly serve the American ideals, they can achieve great things for themselves and the world. This is the lesson we should remember. . . .[33]

In order to remember the lesson of Thomas Jefferson, Gonzalez discovered that he too had to "challenge ancient tyrannies and old customs" and the most effective way of doing so was to run for office.

---

[32] San Antonio Evening News, June 15, 1949.

[33] San Antonio Register, March 12, 1949.

CHAPTER III

REBEL WITH A CAUSE[1]

In 1950 it was generally believed that a candidate of Mexican descent could not win a county-wide election. Students of Bexar County politics did not believe that a Latin American had the political sagacity and resources to conduct an effective campaign, nor did they believe that a Latin American could attract substantial support in rural and suburban areas. Latin-American candidates were often challenged by other Latin Americans at the instigation of Anglo politicians, resulting in a division of votes on the West Side. In other instances, Anglo politicians, using monetary incentives, easily obtained the support of many Latin Americans. Elections were usually won by candidates who received the majority of votes on the North Side, where Latin-American candidates received little support.

Despite the general consensus, there were some skeptics who did not consider it impossible for a Latin American to win. One of these was Henry Gonzalez. His skepticism was based primarily on an analysis of the campaigns of two Latin Americans in 1948. In the Democratic primary of 1948, Assistant District Attorney M. C. Gonzales ran unsuccessfully for the nomination for state representative.

---

[1]Hart Stilwell, "Texas Rebel With a Cause," Coronet, August, 1958, pp. 43-47.

leadership
his involvement
helped.

As attorney for the Mexican Consul General and as a leader in LULAC
and the Mexican Chamber of Commerce, Gonzales was well-known to Latin
Americans. Yet, on the West Side he received relatively little enthusiastic support. This has been attributed to Gonzales' inability to
capture the imagination and confidence of the individual Latin-American
voters. On the other hand, Gonzales, backed by an official endorsement
from organized labor, received creditable support in other areas of
the county. This revealed a potential source of strength for succeed-
ing candidates.

Also in 1948, Gus Garcia was elected to the San Antonio School
Board of Trustees in an election that startled most political observers.
Since the campaign was confined to the school district's boundaries
where many Latin-American families resided, Garcia was able to organize
the area effectively. He was able to draw almost unanimous support
from these families as well as the support of Negroes, most of whom
lived on the East Side. Henry Gonzalez assessed the results of the
two elections and concluded that a Latin American did have an opportunity to win. Gonzalez felt that to win a county-wide election a Latin
American would be compelled to utilize the successful characteristics
of both campaigners; the ability to attract a substantial number of
Anglo votes, and the skill to unite the Latin-American and Negro
minorities.

*strategy
to win*

Armed with the certitude that Latin Americans could win and
with the conviction that San Antonio's minorities needed friendly
representatives in the state legislature, Gonzalez asked two of the

city's Latin-American leaders to run for office. He had been impressed
by their speeches encouraging Latin Americans to pay their poll taxes,
to participate in politics, and to vote for candidates sympathetic to
their needs. They first told him he was "crazy," that a "Mexican"
could not win, and, furthermore, the pay was inadequate. Gonzalez
approached the second leader after hearing him deliver a fire-brand
speech urging Latin Americans to participate in politics. His answer
was similar to the first: "A Mexican can't win, and it doesn't pay
anything." These answers disturbed Gonzalez who could not reconcile
the leaders' public speeches demanding political action with their private statements of defeatism and selfishness. He said that they
"didn't make sense" to him because they "made big speeches about lack
of representation," yet were unwilling to run for office themselves.
Later, Gonzalez returned to talk to one of the leaders to pursue the
matter, but "he got mad" and told him to run himself if he was so
interested. Gonzalez accepted the challenge.[2]

When Gonzalez announced his candidacy for the Democratic nomination for state representative in 1950, he attracted little attention.
He was believed to be another of the Latin Americans whose names occasionally appeared on the ballot, but seldom attracted many votes.
Actually, Gonzalez' announcement marked the beginning of one of the
most remarkable and colorful political careers in Bexar County history.

---

[2]Henry B. Gonzalez, in address to Incarnate Word College Young
Democrats, December 15, 1964.

He was unsuccessful in 1950, but he blazed a path to eventual political triumph for himself and many others of his ethnic origin.

Gonzalez had never actively participated in a political campaign and consequently was naive about practical politics; he didn't
even know the location of the precincts. But Gonzalez did know people,
and they knew him. They knew him as an honest, conscientious, dynamic,
intelligent man and they rallied to support him. Individuals like
Charles De Leon, a grocer, raised campaign funds by sponsoring bingo
games and suppers; Lalo Sólis, a politico of the ward-heeler tradition, helped organize precincts; Mae Waldo, a schoolteacher who was
teaching school with Gonzalez in the veterans' program, spoke in his
behalf at back yard rallies. Parents of juveniles he had helped and
former juveniles who had reached voting age volunteered their help;
fellow members of the Lions, the Eagles, the Organized Voters League,[3]
and the numerous other organizations Gonzalez belonged to pledged
their support. Gonzalez recalls that he was "amazed" to see supporters "everywhere I went."[4]

He based his campaign on, what he called, an urgent need for
"real and true" representation for the "common citizen--the wage
earner." His independence was emphasized by campaign cards which

---

[3]The Organized Voters League was composed of individuals from
the groups that today comprise the liberal faction of the Democratic
Party in Texas--Latin Americans, Negroes, independent liberals, union
members.

[4]Interview with Henry B. Gonzalez, December 15, 1964.

indicated he was "backed by no special interest or pressure group."
He campaigned tirelessly, meeting people day and night. He also
exhibited an enterprising wit when he momentarily integrated the
counter of a segregated drug store. This occurred when he was visiting businesses on East Commerce Street with a Negro friend, Frank
Green, and inadvertently found himself sitting at a drug store counter
with Green. In order not to cause embarrassment, Gonzalez called
aside the owner, whom he knew, and told him Green was not a "real
Negro" but an Ethiopian prince who spoke French but was rapidly learning English. He pleaded that the druggist do nothing to upset the
"prince." After drinking their refreshments, Gonzalez and Green left
and the druggist remained awed that royalty had visited his business.[5]

Aside from a few moments of levity, Gonzalez' campaign was a
serious one. He worked hard to unite the minorities' vote. He adver-
tised in La Prensa that "a vote for Henry B. Gonzalez is one more step
to the unification and defense of nuestra Raza [our race]." Articles
and editorials in his behalf appeared in the Spanish-language newspapers. (In addition to the daily, La Prensa, there were several
Spanish-language periodicals and weeklies.) Alonso Perales, a pioneer
Latin-American leader and noted author, endorsed Gonzalez in his newspaper column as being "wise, dynamic and profoundly interested in our
race." An editorial in La Prensa said Gonzalez' victory would not be
his alone but a collective victory for the Latin-American population.

---

[5]Ibid.

It admired the new face in politics because the old politicos had produced only "bags of tricks with strings attached." Latin Americans
were called upon to unite in a solid bloc for Gonzalez.[6]

Rallies were held where Gonzalez talked of "manpower versus
money power" and decried "discrimination that worked against proper
progress of these 'neglected people.'" He gave impassioned speeches
in both English and Spanish and afterwards the crowds danced and cele-
brated while he shook hands. Money was scarce as the largest single
contributor was Tony Kawazoe, a restaurant owner of Japanese descent,
who donated $50.

Gonzalez' opponents were W. C. "Bill" Bennett, the son of a
county commissioner, and Stanley Banks, Jr., the son of a wealthy
businessman and erstwhile political power. Both opponents offered
"conservative" alternatives to the "progressive" campaign Gonzalez
conducted. On the Sunday before the election Don Politico predicted:
"Gonzalez is pressing for a spot in the run-off with support from
organized labor as well as heavy strength on the West Side."[7]

When election results were tallied, Gonzalez squeezed ahead
of Bennett into a place in the run-off against Banks. Gonzalez carried the West and East Sides solidly in receiving 12,560 votes, 554
more than Bennett; Banks received 15,396 votes to lead the field.

---

[6]Unmarked clippings in Gonzalez' scrapbook.

[7]Don Politico, San Antonio Light, July 21, 1950.

Gonzalez quickly silenced talk of dropping from the run-off by saying:
"I'll continue my fight against the country club set."[8]

Stirred by his sizable vote total, Gonzalez jumped into the
run-off with renewed vigor. He teamed with Maury Maverick, Jr., who
had landed a run-off berth against Frates Seeligson, an established
conservative, and together they campaigned as the voters' "friends."
Gonzalez distributed a pamphlet which boasted that Bexar County's
heart was in the "right place" because, "discarding old, worn-out
prejudices," it gave him "a chance in the run-off" and, "ignoring
costly posters" and a "campaign of malicious rumors," it voted "for a
man--not a name."[9]

However, Bexar County was not quite ready to vote "for a man--
not a name" and in the run-off primary Gonzalez lost by approximately
2,000 votes. Maverick did gain an "upset" victory in defeating Seeligson by little more than 500 votes. In a victory statement, Maverick
said: "I attribute my victory to Henry B. Gonzalez as much as to any
other man in Bexar County."[10] He sent a telegram to Gonzalez in which
he said: "It has been an honor to be associated with you because you
are a brave and first rate man."[11]

---

[8]San Antonio Light, July 24, 1950.

[9]Campaign pamphlet in Gonzalez' scrapbook.

[10]San Antonio Light, August 27, 1950.

[11]Maury Maverick, Jr., telegram to Gonzalez.

In analyzing the outcome, Don Politico stated that "injection of the racial issue into the campaign appeared to solidify the West Side Latin vote" which gave Gonzalez and Maverick large majorities. The anonymous political observer also said that Gonzalez "ran the strongest race of any Latin-American candidate for the legislature in many years."[12]

Gonzalez' strong showing in the legislative race enhanced his political stature. The observation was made that his popularity had grown considerably and his friends would soon insist that he run for office again. But Gonzalez had a family of six children and his primary concern was providing for them. The San Antonio Housing Authority needed someone to take charge of land acquisition and family relocation in connection with new housing projects being built. As a bilingual law graduate, Gonzalez was ideal for the job. Thus in late 1950 he went to work as a civil servant of the City of San Antonio.

Gonzalez has often talked of his job with the Housing Authority. He is still proud of his record of 455 family relocations without an eviction. He was given the opportunity to negotiate with businessmen who had dealings with the Housing Authority and to work with individual families who were affected by the Authority's operations. He served under Mrs. Marie McGuire, now Commissioner of Public Housing. In 1953 he was appointed the first manager of Mirasol Homes, a public housing

---

[12]San Antonio Light, August 27, 1950.

project on the far west of the city. He served as manager for six
months until he resigned to run for the city council in 1953.

The city election of 1953 was perhaps the most expensive municipal election in San Antonio history. Its roots went back to 1951
when, under the lead of Mayor A. C. "Jack" White, the old mayor-
commission form of government was voted out in favor of council-
manager government. The reformist Citizens Committee, financed by
"silk-stocking" money, gained popular support for charter revision.
The city charter was rewritten in the pattern of council-manager government and a Citizens Committee slate of candidates was elected to
the nine council positions.

The new council reelected Jack White mayor and appointed an
out-of-state professional as the new city manager. A council majority
split with Mayor White on a variety of subjects including the manager's
salary. When the council majority voted to annex large portions of
land to extend the city limits, they included the home of millionaire-
oilman Al Jergins. For reasons that only he knows, Jergins joined
with White and helped finance an anti-administration ticket called the
San Antonians. Millionaire Jergins was determined to defeat the incum-
bents and, consequently, looked for a cross-section of potential candidates who could contribute to a victory. Jergins was not an active
politician but he did possess a keen political sense, and he had been
impressed by the Gonzalez campaign in 1950. Gonzalez was asked to run
with the San Antonians just six months after he had become manager of
Mirasol Homes.

There was little need to encourage Gonzalez to run since he had been heartened by his run-off campaign in 1950 and he now saw the opportunity for victory in the city council election. Yet he hesitated because he could not afford to give up his job, which he would be forced to do if he became a candidate. Sensing his dilemma, partisans of the Citizens Committee attempted to persuade Gonzalez that he should not risk or forfeit his job with the Housing Authority. This convinced Gonzalez to run for the council as he now saw a special challenge in accepting the invitation to run with the San Antonians. (It should be noted here that, when Gonzalez is seriously debating a question within himself, an attempt to pressure him into a particular decision will usually convince him to make an opposing decision. He reacts negatively to pressure of any kind, especially when it is in the form of thinly-veiled threats.)

He became "titular head of the West Side campaign" for the San Antonians. Of the nine candidates on the ticket, he was the only Latin American; the Citizens Committee had two Latin Americans, incumbent Ruben Lozano and Gonzalez' opponent, George de la Garza, an automobile salesman.

Since the Citizens Committee had two Latin-American candidates, the San Antonians were compelled to use a technique other than ethnic loyalty to capture the West Side vote. The answer was left to Gonzalez who was popular and well-known among Latin Americans. Money for television and radio was readily available and Gonzalez made good use of it. Over Spanish-language stations, he assured voters that the San

Antonians would properly represent and listen to the problems of the West Side. On television he blossomed into a unique San Antonian proponent as he adapted to the new method of campaigning like a "duck to water." He campaigned particularly hard for Mrs. E. M. Stevens, Lozano's opponent, by reminding Latin Americans of some uncomplimentary remarks Lozano had made discrediting the initiative and education of the ordinary "Mexicano." There were few voters who did not know that Gonzalez was a candidate, as they were constantly reminded by their children saying: "And Gonzalez toooo." The phrase was from a campaign jingle that named the first eight candidates and then, in a Spanish accent, reminded the listeners that Gonzalez also was a candidate. Inspired by Gonzalez himself, the gimmick proved invaluable to the San Antonians.[13]

Mayor White and Gonzalez won the election by clear majorities, while the seven other San Antonians landed in a run-off against their Citizens Committee opponents. Gonzalez soundly defeated de la Garza on the West Side, and Mrs. Stevens did surprisingly well in this area against Lozano.

The Citizens Committee campaign manager concluded that the White and Gonzalez victories resulted from "substantial majorities in the old-line machine areas." He expressed disappointment in the light North Side turnout which normally favored the Citizens. But he displayed confidence that the "alarming surge of strength in the old-line

---

[13]Don Politico, San Antonio Light, May 15, 1953.

machine areas will once again arouse the crusading spirit [of] the good government forces."[14]

The "old-line machine areas" referred to were the West and East Sides of the city where the San Antonians had gained substantial majorities. However, it was generally conceded that a major reason for these majorities was not that the areas were under machine control, but that Henry Gonzalez was an effective campaigner. He was considered "a young man with a razor-sharp wit and a wide smile," who had been "catching the public eye for some time." Gonzalez had "bugged eyes a bit by . . . going into a run-off with Representative Stanley Banks, Jr., in 1950," and had impressed people as "one of the top personalities of the campaign from the first television rally of the San Antonians."[15]

During the campaign Gonzalez had provided laughs with his "off-the-cuff campaign sallies," but had become "dead serious when pledging he would represent all the people of San Antonio." Voters were assured that "he knows West Side problems" and would not "hesitate to speak out on them."[16]

In the run-off he worked diligently for the election of the other ticket members. He again appeared on television and made radio-broadcasts, in both Spanish and English, in behalf of the San Antonians.

---

[14]San Antonio Light, April 10, 1953.

[15]San Antonio Light, April 8, 1953.

[16]Ibid.

He concentrated on the political weaknesses of Ruben Lozano and spoke
ceaselessly for Mrs. Stevens. The San Antonians were successful in
the run-off as they defeated all seven remaining Citizens Committee
candidates. The council then elected Jack White mayor, and Gonzalez
as mayor pro-tem. For his tireless work, his colleagues rewarded him
with their confidence. He was moved by their action and told them:
"What a landmark you have made, designating me your mayor pro-tem. In
doing so you have stamped out the big lie that this country is the
downtrodder of minorities "[17] His acceptance speech brought him
acknowledgments from even Europe and Asia and marked the beginning of
a fruitful career in elected office. He quickly became a hard-working
member of the council devoting full time to a position that paid only
$20 a meeting and no more than $1,040 a year. He supplemented his
income by continuing his translating business, but a constant flow of
troubled constituents into the Houston Building office gave him little
time for business endeavors. During his years on the city council
Gonzalez and his family lived a frugal life. He relied heavily on
assistance from his father, his brother Joaquin, and on a series of
promissory notes.

Although the pay was poor, the "water was fine." Gonzalez now
had a forum from which to present his views, and the opportunity to
represent the "common citizen" in the manner he believed proper.

---

[17]San Antonio News, May 1, 1953.

Two weeks after taking office, Gonzalez attracted banner headlines by opposing a proposition by the mayor and city manager to "burn
communist-tinged" books in the public library. He called the proposal
a "tempest in a teapot" and said he did not favor "labeling, much less
burning books--particularly when the burning smells of Hitler tactics."[18] The proposal raised the ire of many citizens, including the
chairman of the library board, M. M. Harris, who was also Editor of the
San Antonio Express.

For the remainder of their term the San Antonians found little
they could agree upon. Since they had incurred the wrath of newsmen,
press coverage was unfavorable. However, Gonzalez became a press personality with a finely developed sense of timing and perceptiveness.
His name became a household word as he fulfilled a "self-dedicated"
mission of "protecting the minority in matters of culture as well as
economy."[19]

He captured newspaper headlines when he warned of a mounting
vice problem in San Antonio and told of an attempted bribe to keep him
quiet. Statewide attention was given to his disclosure that he had
been denied use of a picnic area in an adjoining county because he was
of Mexican descent. Although officially nothing was done to correct
this discriminatory action, San Antonio residents were impressed that

---

[18] San Antonio News, May 15, 1953.

[19] Ken McClure, moderator of weekly radio program "Your City
Government," (transcript) June 12, 1953.

a serious problem still existed. When the City Water Board announced
a water rate increase, Gonzalez insisted on a thorough investigation
of the feasibility of the rate hikes.

He answered critics who accused him of "headline hunting" by
quoting Charles Peguy, the French philosopher: "He who failed to bel-
low the truth when he knew the truth is an accomplice of liars and
cheats." He said: "I firmly believe in this dictum and so I will
always speak out when armed with the truth."[20] His answer was accen-
tuated when he added: "I, for one, like to be recognized when I do
good work. When I do bad, regardless of my personal sentiments, I
should be exposed. Those who charge me with publicity seeking actually
magnify my figure."[21]

As mayor pro-tem, Gonzalez was called upon to attend numerous
functions as the city's representative. When he went to these activities he usually wore white shoes and, many times, a white suit. He
always stood out in a crowd as people gathered around him. He developed
a magnetic quality that proved extremely helpful in future campaigns.
When dignitaries from Mexico visited San Antonio, Gonzalez conversed
with them in their native language. He became the champion of the
"little man," as he always devoted a compassionate ear to anyone with
a problem.

---

[20]Henry B. Gonzalez, from transcript of KTSA radio program,
July 10, 1953.

[21]San Antonio Light, August 6, 1953.

Privately, some of the businessmen who had supported the San Antonians were distressed with Gonzalez. His statements concerning equality, water rates, and other topics were arousing the people and giving the Citizens Committee, which was still active, propaganda material for the next election. A recall movement against him was discussed. It was hinted that he could resign and find attractive employment but this confirmed his decision to stay on. This was not an easy decision for him since his family was in financial straits. In fact, at a later time he publicly announced that he was considering resigning for financial reasons.

When he announced his financial dilemma, fellow councilmen expressed opinions much like those of Councilman Raymond Russell who said: "He has worked hard and has done a good job and besides he makes the rest of us think."[22] A local political writer referred to him as "stormy, brilliant councilman Henry B. Gonzalez, the first genuine, Grade-A 'poor man' ever elected to a local managerite council," and suggested that strong consideration be given to raising councilmen's remuneration.[23] However, Gonzalez survived the financial crisis with the help of his brother Joaquin and remained on the council. Since then his annual income has been a major question in his political campaigns.

---

[22]San Antonio Express, December 7, 1953.

[23]Jon Ford, "Backstage in Politics," San Antonio Express, December 6, 1953.

In the latter half of their two-year term the San Antonians became more and more involved in bitter struggles and failed to legislate for proper governing of the city. City managers were hired and fired, and other key city employees resigned or were dismissed. Council-manager government was undergoing a serious test as the people tired of the council's antics. A movement to recall six councilmen was organized and editorials called on "decent citizens" to recall "White's Wrecking Crew." Gonzalez was listed as one of only three councilmen who "have demonstrated any semblance of responsibility."[24]

An example of this "responsibility" was Gonzalez' effort to expose a minimum-standards housing ordinance which he said, "seems to make poor people illegal without offering a way out." He was given credit for "shooting" the proposed ordinance "so full of holes that only its 'mother' could love it."[25] When the telephone :company proposed a raise in phone rates, Gonzalez studied the request in depth with an accountant friend and submitted a detailed, nine-page counterproposal. His plan reduced the rate increase considerably, but still gave the company a fair return. In addition, he called for the establishment of a city utilities department under provisions of the city charter.

[24]San Antonio News, August 10, 1954.

[25]Bill Reddell, "The Bill Board," San Antonio Express, April 9, 1954.

These and other actions brought Gonzalez to an open clash with
the White faction of the council. This came after the recall movement
gained momentum and the affected councilmen were resigning as a consequence. To fill one vacancy, the White faction appointed Herbert
Schenker, a political ally of Jack White. Gonzalez accused Schenker
of taking the oath of office illegally because he had previously promised the city manager position to Dr. G. A. Ross. This promise, Gonzalez said, was in violation of the city charter. Schenker did not
remain on the council long, but he did cause Gonzalez much difficulty.

The new councilman accused Gonzalez of practing law without a
license and exhibited notarized statements from two individuals who
alleged this as fact. Gonzalez denied the charge, sought the individuals who made the statements, and obtained affidavits from them stating
they had falsely signed the accusations on the promise that help would
be obtained in keeping a relative from going to prison. The individuals
appeared at a city council meeting to verify their second statement.
Gonzalez maintained that the allegation was part of a conspiracy to
discredit his integrity and remove him from the council. In addition
to this episode, his background was thoroughly investigated, all
hotels and motels in the city were checked for embarrassing evidence,
and harrassing phone calls were made to him in the middle of the night.
He eliminated the phone calls by yelling shrilly into the phone one
night--no one ever called after that.

A remarkable ability to "call a spade a joke" has allowed Gonzalez to remain in politics. Although he has often been angered

always calm & collected

momentarily by statements or actions of individuals, he has always managed to maintain his composure and to insert humor into the circumstances. For instance, during the serious crisis of the Schenker
affair, when private detectives and others were investigating him,
Gonzalez contrived a plan to advise the opposition he was willing to
play their game. He arranged with a friend to invite some councilmen
to a formal reception on behalf of the mayor. These guests were
invited at the last moment, but were assured that it was important to
the mayor that they attend. When the guests arrived, in formal attire,
at the White Plaza Hotel (owned by Mayor White) they went to the desig-
nated room but found no reception. Gonzalez was across the street
amusedly viewing the whole affair. He gained new strength from this
experience.

The ill-fated San Antonians were removed from influence when
five of the councilmen who were recall targets resigned. A few months
later the Good Government League (GGL) was organized by citizens who,
this observer believes, were remnants of the Citizens Committee, and
announced a slate of candidates for city council. Although not a member of the GGL ticket, Gonzalez was unopposed by their forces. Newspaper articles indicated that Gonzales was approached by both the GGL
and the rival People's ticket to run on their slates. However, Gonzalez announced for reelection as an independent. He admitted his

strength was "in the east and west" and said, "I'll run again and make a good showing."[26]

Gonzalez entered his third political campaign against four opponents. One was Joe Menchaca who distributed leaflets that asked: "What has the NAACP given Henry Gonzalez to stir up racial strife in San Antonio?" The second was Paul Halbert of the People's ticket. Another was Bruce Woodward who accused Gonzalez of being unreliable since he was not a successful businessman. The fourth candidate was Dr. Therold Berry, a dentist, who was the nephew of V. E. "Red" Berry[27] and who received financial and other support from his uncle. A campaign newspaper was distributed by Berry accusing Gonzalez of being a "cunning left wing politician" who had attempted to place Negro "left wing policy king" Valmo Bellinger and Negro "left wing meddler" G. J. Sutton on the city council. (This referred to Gonzalez' efforts to name Sutton and Bellinger to replace resigning San Antonian councilmen.) The newspaper also contained several other uncomplimentary statements concerning Gonzalez' moral character.[28]

Refusing to be placed on the defensive, Gonzalez answered the accusations as he has answered others--by ignoring them and running on his record. As an independent he was on a limited budget. Funds were

---

[26]Paul Thompson, "Top of the News," San Antonio News, December 9, 1954.

[27]Above, p. 20.

[28]Newspaper in Gonzalez' scrapbook.

raised through bingos, suppers, raffles, and small direct contributions. He was able to buy some television time and made effective use
of this medium. He was now a polished television performer and he
spoke effectively without notes or cue cards. Berry blanketed the com-
munications media with spot announcements and half-hour programs.
There were signs that Berry would be successful in arousing hidden
prejudices in many people.

A sworn pledge was made by Gonzalez to uphold and work for the
planks of his platform. He defended council-manager government, empha-
sizing the line of demarcation between administrative (city manager)
and policy-making (city council) decisions; he pledged to work in harmony with responsible colleagues; and he promised to maintain an "open
door" to citizens and groups from all sections of the city. He acknowledged that he had abstained from voting on some issues as a matter of
principle. He emphasized that he would always abstain when asked to
make a hurried decision on legislation "that was unfounded, ridiculous
and incomplete as to facts."[29]

The campaign reached a dangerous climax when unidentified persons shot at Gonzalez one evening as he was walking into his house from
the garage. The bullets went wide of their mark, but they did remind
Gonzalez that he was in a serious and dangerous campaign. He decided
not to reveal the incident so that it would not influence the election.
Apparently there was no need to reveal the shooting as Gonzalez won

---

[29]Copy of Platform in Gonzalez' scrapbook.

without a run-off. He gained a clear majority of almost 2,000 over the 4 opponents. For the first time in his career he carried several North Side boxes. Moreover, because the turnout on the West Side was very poor, his election was insured by the vote on the North Side.

During the campaign Gonzalez had been endorsed by the San Antonio Express and News for his efforts to maintain responsible council-manager government. After his election the newspaper acclaimed his victory for the same reason and applauded Gonzalez as the first independent to win a council seat under the existing charter. He was the lone survivor of the ill-fated San Antonian ticket.

While the San Antonians appeared never to agree on matters before the council, the Good Government Leaguers appeared never to disagree. Once again Gonzalez assumed the familiar role of dissenter and constructive irritant. He called for a tax rate reduction, and again opposed water rate hikes unless the need was fully investigated. His stand on public utilities was explained when he said that they "stand apart from private business and in exchange for the monopoly they enjoy, must submit to regulation and reflect the public's desires."[30]

Throughout his years on the council Gonzalez spoke against segregation in general and specifically against city segregation of public facilities. In early 1956 he offered ordinances desegregating all city facilities and the council passed them. This remains as one

---

[30] San Antonio Express, August 8, 1955.

one of his proudest achievements. Repeal of the segregation ordinances
also marked a turning point in Gonzalez' career. He began to note
that the new council was making sincere efforts to help all sections
of the city and only time would reveal their success.

Time, however, was catching up with Gonzalez as he approached
his fortieth birthday. He felt it time to move up or out of politics.
There were other peaks to climb and uncharted waters to explore. On
his fortieth birthday, Gonzalez decided to run for the Texas Senate
and announced his decision. He felt that many of the state's crucial
problems "have been postponed too long" and that "some action must be
taken" on them.[31]

Fellow councilmen showered Gonzalez with verbal tributes
praising him for an outstanding job and for his dedication to hard work
without monetary return. Mayor Edwin Kuykendall thanked Gonzalez for
having "inspired me many times," and praised him as a "man of conviction." City Manager Steve Matthews told him "you have given me the
opportunity to be a better man."[32] The councilmen then reached into
their pockets and raised $100, enough for the filing fee.

Paul Thompson, a newspaper columnist who often had long conversations with Gonzalez, described the retiring councilman as an officeholder who

---

[31]San Antonio Light, May 3, 1956.

[32]Ibid.

has freely expressed opinions on a phenomenal range of topics. He
talks fluently and well gets [sic] more footage in the newspapers
than any senator or congressman. Underneath it all he's a goodhearted boy with a real desire to improve the community, especially
the Latin American part of it.[33]

The fluent "goodhearted boy" was now in a campaign that was
self-admittedly "do or die." His opponent was the incumbent, Senator
O. F. "Ozzie" Lattimer who, while not a spectacular campaigner, was
experienced and entrenched. Don Politico admitted that Gonzalez had
proved his capability of "piling up a big city-wide vote" and usually
had been "in tune with the thoughts of the voters."[34] Thompson
revealed that while some Good Government League leaders were talking
against Gonzalez as being "too vocal" for the Senate, he had "shown an
aptitude for picking up 'moderate' north and south end votes."[35]

In the six years from his initial political campaign to his
decision to run for state senator, Gonzalez matured into a seasoned and
astute politician and demonstrated a unique sense of devotion to the
public he represented. He was a full-time councilman as he studied
and mastered city budgetary procedures and other municipal functions.
In addition, he devoted much time listening to and attempting to help
constituents who sought his assistance. When he resigned from the
council there were few, if any, aspects of San Antonio city government

---

[33]Paul Thompson, "Top of the News," San Antonio News, May 3,
1956.

[34]Don Politico, San Antonio Light, May 4, 1956.

[35]Paul Thompson, "Top of the News," San Antonio News, May 11,
1956.

with which he was not thoroughly familiar. Undoubtedly, he believed
that he was well-qualified to move up the political ladder to a legislative position in state government.

However, for almost two decades Bexar County's legislative
delegation had been dominated by representatives of the conservative
political tradition. Most members of the business community were of
the same conservative tradition and the incumbent candidates for
reelection usually had little difficulty in raising campaign funds when
challenged by liberal candidates. In 1952 the county voted for Republican Dwight Eisenhower and most forecasters predicted a similar outcome in 1956. Any candidate opposing an incumbent state legislator
was faced with an uphill battle and could look forward to few funds
with which to campaign. Henry Gonzalez had one additional handicap--
he was a Latin American, and this was a county-wide primary.

The District Clerk estimated that of the 140,000 eligible
voters in Bexar County 100,500 were Anglos, while only 29,000 were
Latin Americans and 10,500 were Negroes.[36] These figures indicate, of
course, that, in order to win, Gonzalez would have to rely heavily on
Anglos to vote for "a man--not a name." He campaigned relentlessly,
relying on volunteers to distribute material and on testimonial din-
ners to raise funds. He called his opponent a "do-nothing senator"
and asked for the opportunity to work hard in the State Senate.

---

[36]Don Politico, San Antonio Light, May 20, 1956.

Television was used sparingly but effectively as Gonzalez' acknowledged skill again proved successful.

Voter interest on the West Side, where Gonzalez was a solid favorite, was intensified by an extensive campaign by attorney Albert Peña, Jr. for county commissioner of precinct one. His campaign organization covered every section of the precinct in behalf of both Peña and Gonzalez. (Gonzalez has never campaigned within the framework of a tightly-knit organization and has always run independently, accepting equally the assistance of individual volunteers and organizations alike; Peña, on the other hand, is strictly an organization man who relies heavily and almost exclusively on one for assistance.)

Gonzalez defeated Lattimer by only 282 votes. The large majorities Lattimer expected to garner on the North and South Sides of the city did not materialize. Gonzalez was able to capture as much as 40 per cent of the vote in several North Side precincts which, when added to an overwhelming vote on the West and East Sides, proved sufficient to win the primary. The victory was called a "staggering upset against long odds," and was credited in part to Gonzalez' "personality and relentless drive."[37]

The Republican Party of Bexar County gave Gonzalez little time to celebrate his win, as it quickly announced that a Republican would oppose Gonzalez in the General Election. The first candidate,

---

[37]Paul Thompson, "Top of the News," San Antonio News, July 30, 1956.

seventy-year-old attorney Neil Barton, withdrew and was replaced by attorney Jesse Oppenheimer who had resigned an executive position with a manufacturing firm to make the race. His announced intention for running was to help establish a two party system in Texas. He admitted, however, that Republicans would not have opposed Lattimer.

The campaign proved to be bitter and sensational. Gonzalez charged that the interests that backed Democrat Lattimer were now backing Republican Oppenheimer and that their motives were prompted not by party loyalty, but by personal animosity. Gonzalez was the only local candidate with Republican opposition and consequently was able to point out that a sincere two party system could not be established by "ganging-up" on one candidate. Oppenheimer accused Gonzalez of being a "leftist," "left-winger," and a "creeping socialist." Gonzalez countered that he was a right handed pitcher and therefore a "right-winger" and that the only thing "creeping" about him were his "shorts." Again, his engaging wit proved invaluable in a campaign. Yet, Oppenheimer repeatedly attempted to depict Gonzalez as a radical outside of the main stream of San Antonio politics. He warned of the dangers of electing a liberal such as Gonzalez. In answer, Gonzalez gave his own definition of liberal: "I mean by liberal, a man who believes in living and let live, in toleration, a person not dogmatic. If that's what liberal means, I'm proud to be called one."[38]

---

[38]San Antonio Light, October 19, 1956.

In the General Election, Eisenhower carried Bexar County by a margin greater than in 1952. Gonzalez defeated Oppenheimer by approximately 13,000 votes and ran only 6,000 behind Eisenhower. On the West Side Gonzalez' margin was almost 10,000 where he ran more than 2,000 votes ahead of Adlai Stevenson.[39] The coattail theory was reversed in San Antonio as the national ticket trailed Gonzalez. The key to Gonzalez' success in the election is dramatized by these figures since his margin on the West Side provided almost all of his margin of victory as he was able to neutralize his opponent in the other areas of the county. This show of strength made him the first elected Latin American state senator in Texas history. (Antonio Navarro, a native Texan of Spanish-Italian descent was appointed state senator in 1846 and served one term.) One paper called his victory "a just reward for worthy public service."[40]

Gonzalez spent five years in the Texas Senate and left an indelible impression on state politics. He became a symbol of the rewards that come to a politician who places principle above personal gain. He opened the minds of thousands of Texans who impulsively believed in segregation. He helped give an articulate, intelligent, and witty voice to the liberal tradition of Texas. He gave effective voice to the "common citizen" he had first campaigned for in 1950. To

---

[39]San Antonio Light, November 7, 1956.

[40]San Antonio News, November 8, 1956.

do this he first had to gain the respect of his Senate colleagues--his peers.

There is little doubt that many Bexar County citizens were shocked when Gonzalez was elected senator. In one instance, Gonzalez overheard a woman lawyer assure a friend: "I'm not going to have that Mexican represent me in Austin." She was surprised to hear him answer, "Relax lady, you have him." One man on a city council of nine men was one thing, but in the Senate one man represented the entire county which constitutes the twenty-sixth senatorial district. There was disbelief in some quarters that a "Mexican" was now their state senator. This attitude was reflected in the Capitol itself as some senators and other state officials referred to Gonzalez as "that Mexican."[41] But he had penetrated barriers like this before; all he needed was a little time.

At the age of forty, Gonzalez began a five-year stint in the State Senate. He moved cautiously at first, attempting to learn the rules and customs of the Senate. He introduced legislative measures that his experiences in San Antonio led him to believe were necessary. Bills he introduced concerned a domestic relations court for Bexar County; establishment of a medical school in San Antonio; strict lobby control and registration; a state minimum wage of forty cents per hour; provisions for open meetings by state and local public agencies; party identification to prevent party jumping in primaries; a public

---

[41]From unmarked clipping in Gonzalez' scrapbook.

defender office for Bexar County. He authored a law authorizing urban renewal in San Antonio. A total of eighteen bills which he sponsored, co-sponsored or handled in the Senate became law.

However, Gonzalez' conviction to "always speak out when armed with the truth" was the force that firmly established his place in the Senate and, in this writer's opinion, in the annals of Texas history. The many years of constant pursuit of the teachings and writings of the scholars of the Western World coupled with his own experiences as a member of a minority ethnic group enabled Gonzalez to fluently and intelligently tell the people of Texas of the evils of segregation and the folly of ten segregation bills introduced in the Legislature. Without Gonzalez' tenacious intellectual preparation; without his experiences as part of a minority group; without his election to the State Senate; and indeed, without his decision to use the filibuster as a forum to "speak the truth," Texas could well have reverted to the degenerate atmosphere on human relations that now plagues Mississippi and Alabama.

In 1957 ten bills aimed at circumventing the United States Supreme Court's decision in the Brown v. Board of Education segregation case were introduced in the Legislature. These bills had the tacit approval of Governor Price Daniel. They ranged from one that called for local option elections for determining school board policy on integration to one that denied public employment to members of the National Association for the Advancement of Colored People (NAACP). On May 2, 1957, five months after freshman Senator Gonzalez had first stepped up to the Senate floor, the first of these bills to pass the House of Representatives was sent to the Senate. The bill allowed placement of school children for reasons other than color and included provisions for mental agility tests to be given to determine placement.

Prior to House passage of the bill, Gonzalez and Senator Abraham "Chick" Kazen of Laredo had warned that they would filibuster any segregation bill presented to the Senate. When the House bill reached the Senate floor, Kazen, son of Lebanese immigrants, gained the floor and began a fifteen-hour filibuster. He methodically dissected the bill, pointed out its flaws, and chastised the Legislature for attempting to circumvent the "law of the land." Kazen was assisted by long questions from Gonzalez and a few friendly senators.

When Kazen began to tire, Gonzalez took the floor and held it for twenty-one hours and two minutes. He asked whether Texas liberty was only the liberty of Anglo-Saxons. Words, phrases, thoughts, and ideals he had acquired through prolific reading since childhood flowed into the Senate chamber as "he moved from one topic to another with no strain or pause," always keeping "close to the point at issue."[42] He told of his experiences as a member of a minority group and he said that the bill could be used against Latin Americans as well as Negroes.

Time reported that "time and again he warned his colleagues of the ultimate perils of segregation: 'It may be some can chloroform their conscience. But if we fear long enough, we hate, and if we hate

---

[42]Paul Thompson. "Top of the News," San Antonio News, May 3, 1957.

long enough, we fight.'" The national magazine also quoted Gonzalez
in a passage that dramatized the issue:

> The assault on the inward dignity of man which our society pro-
> tects, has been made. And this . . . is an assault on the very
> idea of America, which began as a new land of hope. . . . For whom
> does the bell toll? You, the white man, think it tolls for the
> Negroes. I say, the bell tolls for you. It is ringing for all of
> us.[43]

Almost every newspaper in Texas reported the filibuster on
their front pages with banner headlines. National magazines and news
commentators devoted attention to the Kazen-Gonzalez talkathon which
lasted thirty-six hours and two minutes and kept the Senate in session
for the longest continuous period in Texas history. There is no doubt
that the filibuster provided a dramatic setting for discussion of the
most crucial issue of mid-twentieth century American politics. Gonzalez did not have the votes to kill the race bills, but he did have a
forum to speak out against them. Newspapers reported how he discussed
the issue of integration, quoting the views of the great thinkers of
civilization on equality and justice. It is difficult to imagine that
any but the most unreasonable minds did not seriously examine their
views on racial segregation. It is certain that the Senate leadership
reconsidered its plan to pass all ten bills, as only two were brought
to the floor for votes. Gonzalez and Kazen succeeded in killing the
bills armed with only the filibuster and the firm conviction that

---

[43]"Texas: For Whom the Bells Toll," Time, May 13, 1957, p. 27.

segregation was morally wrong. To emphasize his determination, Gonzalez
filibustered a second time against segregation for eleven hours.

In a sense, the filibusters provided a storm signal for the
non-violent resistence movement which has enveloped the South in the
1960's. Texas was the only state of the old Confederacy that could
have provided a dramatic and official forum to speak out against segregation. Mississippi would not have tolerated it, nor Alabama and the
other eight Southern states. A state legislator from these states
could not have filibustered without fear of possible physical and certain electoral reprisal. Yet, Gonzalez, aside from a few isolated
cases, received the support of his home district including editorial
backing. He assumed the responsibility of registering "the dumb protest, of the inarticulate," because he felt the duty to do so.[44] And,
in doing so, he gave Negroes and every other minority a voice within
the sanctity of a Southern legislative chamber.

Gonzalez' uncompromising stand on segregation lifted him into
a position of state-wide prominence. He received the state NAACP
"Citizenship Award" and was named the outstanding Latin American Citizen of the Year by The Alba Club of The University of Texas. He
accepted speaking engagements all over the state and became the
acknowledged "symbolic leader" of Texas' "combined Latin and Negro

---

[44]Henry B. Gonzalez, during the filibuster, as quoted in
"Gonzalez for Governor" brochure, 1958.

minorities of two and a half million."[45] Newspapers throughout the
state referred to him as "liberal Senator Gonzalez."

In the Senate he tangled with Governor Daniel twice during a
special session. The first was over the appointment of Joe Frazier
Brown to the judgeship of the new 150th District Court which Gonzalez
had successfully fought for in the Senate after some verbal jousts
with the San Antonio Bar Association. The Bar favored establishment
of a district court instead of the domestic relations court that Gonzalez was attempting to establish. After arriving at an agreement
that the new district court would handle matters involving juvenile
and domestic cases involving children, the court bill was passed into
law. Daniel appointed Brown to the judgeship without properly consulting Gonzalez whose "advise and consent" was needed according to senatorial custom. The senator felt the appointment to be a personal
affront since he had advised Daniel before the appointment that Brown
was not a suitable candidate.

Amid enormous pressures created primarily by the editorial and
news coverage of the San Antonio Express and News, Gonzalez refused to
accept the Brown appointment and advised his Senate colleagues that
Brown was "personally obnoxious" to him. After a closed door session
the Senate accepted Gonzalez' objection and refused to consent to the
appointment. Reaction to this in two San Antonio newspapers was

---

[45]Ronnie Dugger, "Filibusters and Majority Rule," The Progressive, August, 1957, p. 21.

vehement as they concluded that Gonzalez had placed his political career in jeopardy.

Gonzalez, however, denounced pressures against him and said that he had "not abandoned the office to accept the views of anyone else" and reflected that "some people think they are the Senator from Bexar County."[46]

At least one political reporter concluded, even before the eventual showdown on the Brown appointment, that "although a lot of people can't quite get used to the idea, Gonzalez is starting to insist on being treated like a senator."[47] After Brown's rejection the Light reported in a headline: "Daniel Finds Gonzalez Can't be Pressured."[48]

The second confrontation with Daniel was over the "Troop bill" which gave the governor authority to close schools where there was threat of violence and the possibility of federal troops being called in. This was shortly after the Little Rock school crisis in Arkansas. Gonzalez filibustered against the bill for twenty hours, accusing Daniel of seeking powers to make himself "czar of school districts." Daniel countered by appearing on state-wide television in support of the "Troop bill" and denouncing Gonzalez' stand. The bill passed, but

---

[46]San Antonio Light, November 8, 1957.

[47]Jon Ford, "Capitol Notebook," San Antonio Express, October 31, 1957.

[48]San Antonio Light, November 8, 1957.

again Gonzalez had directed state-wide attention to the segregation issue.

In 1958 forces of the Democrats of Texas (DOT), an organization of liberals, attempted to find an opponent for Daniel in the Democratic primary. Gonzalez' name was mentioned first as a possible candidate for lieutenant governor, but he stopped these rumors by saying that the lieutenant governor's mansion was not big enough for his family of eight children., His name was then mentioned as a candidate for governor. At first he denied the possibility, but when no major opponent other than former Governor W. Lee O'Daniel announced against Daniel, Gonzalez decided to enter the race.

From the very beginning there was little hope of success as he was a Latin American, a liberal, and a Catholic, and Daniel was running for a traditional second term. He announced, however, that his purpose in running was to afford an alternative to the existing choice between "Tweedle dee dee and O'Tweedle dee dee." He said voters at least should be able to choose "Tweedle dee dum." He argued that "no one should win by default" and every candidate should be forced to take stands on issues that otherwise might be avoided. His candidacy attracted major news coverage and he was offered the opportunity to discuss the issues as he saw them.

Despite his efforts to offer an alternative, he failed to gain the official endorsement of labor unions and DOT. These groups reasoned that discretion was the better part of valor and their weak position in state politics would be weakened even more if they supported Gonzalez. They also felt that the chances of Senator Ralph Yarborough's reelection would suffer. Many individual members of the two groups campaigned for Gonzalez but not with official sanction. Their position was much like an East Texas union man's, who explained: "I'm going to vote for Henry Gonzalez, but I won't endorse him."[49]

Gonzalez traversed the state several times, severely criticizing Daniel for his failure to provide leadership in state government. He endorsed federal aid for school lunches; opposed a sales or income tax; called for elimination of college tuition; supported increase in expenditures for upkeep of mental, tubercular, and other health facilities whose patients, he said, could not afford a lobby; asked for a youth conservation program; favored tax on natural gas pipelines; and, in all sections of the state including East Texas, he asked that the "law of the land" be obeyed in respect to school segregation. These were positions that no major candidate in Texas could espouse and still expect to win. Yet, he was accepted as a major candidate and given the corresponding news coverage. Because he did not expect to win he was not burdened with the shackles that keep most major candidates from speaking out--the fear of offending one group or another, especially major campaign contributors.

The state senator did not accept large campaign contributions from individual sources because of the acknowledged strings attached to such donations. (This writer is personally aware of contributions

---

[49]Unmarked clipping in Gonzalez' scrapbook.

Gonzalez has refused since the gubernatorial campaign for the same reason.) He spent only $17,000 in the race while Daniel spent $91,000.[50] There was never an actual state campaign headquarters since Gonzalez had limited campaign funds. Some supporters found it difficult to understand Gonzalez' lack of emphasis on a central campaign organization, and felt he was diminishing his already poor likelihood of winning. However, Gonzalez has always been an independent campaigner who personally directs and manages every aspect of his own campaigns. In a state-wide campaign the disadvantages arising from this arrangement are obvious. But Gonzalez had no false illusions of winning and did not want to be saddled with unpaid expenses he would be responsible for after the election.

Governor Daniel received 60 per cent of the total vote and won easily without a run-off. Gonzalez polled less than 19 per cent of the vote, but ran ahead of O'Daniel by capturing creditable totals in the urban areas and winning 11 counties, mostly in South Texas. (A fourth candidate received approximately 30,000 votes.) In this area there lived a large number of Latin Americans who usually voted in conformity with the dictates of political bosses. In 1958 South Texas political machines did not endorse Gonzalez, yet he carried the area nevertheless, leading some observers to conclude that Latin-American voters were entering a new political phase.

---

[50]Fred Gantt, Jr., The Chief Executive in Texas (Austin: The University of Texas Press, 1964), p. 278.

In 1959 Gonzalez returned to Austin for the regular session of
the 57th Legislature. Although he had lost the election for governor,
his colleagues accepted him in a manner much different from his first
year in the Senate. There was no longer mention of "that Mexican" and
even political opponents greeted him warmly. However, this was not
the case with six members of Bexar County's delegation in the House
who campaigned as members of the conservative Bexar Legislative Group
during the 1958 primaries. Speculation was quickly opened as to which
of the six would challenge Gonzalez in 1960. When Gonzalez wrote constituents in critical terms of a central licensing bill sponsored by
Representative Frates Seeligson, the representative retorted that he
had "never liked Henry politically, and after this, I don't believe I
like him personally."[51]

Despite the dichotomy in political philosophy between six
Bexar legislators and Gonzalez and freshman Representative Franklin
Spears, the delegation was able to unite and obtain passage of a medical school bill that culminated a twelve-year struggle. Gonzalez was
able to achieve the passage of the bill in the Senate by a twenty-five
to four vote, despite active opposition from Senator Charles Herring
who wanted the school in Austin. The one-sided vote was called "one
of the overlooked political coups of the regular session." It also
indicated the legislative finesse that Gonzalez was developing since

[51]San Antonio Express, April 14, 1959.

some of his votes came from East Texas senators who had apparently
"finally made an adjustment to Henry."[52]

In two bills concerning the San Antonio water problem, Gonzalez effectively demonstrated a determined conviction of opposition
to the creation of new taxing bodies, particularly those not directly
responsible to voters. The San Antonio River Authority (SARA)
requested the power to levy taxes to raise necessary revenues to continue flood control projects. Gonzalez opposed the plan unless the
board of directors was selected by election rather than by appointment
by the governor and the Authority's books were subject to periodic
auditing. He also criticized SARA's policy of employing conservative
Representative Marshall Bell on a $100 monthly retainer which he
called a clear case of conflict of interest. In other actions he managed to delete the taxing section from a bill to establish the Edwards
Underground Water District; to require that its board directors be
elected; and to provide for regular audits. Gonzalez' reasoning
behind this stand can be detected in a statement concerning the SARA
issue: "The small homeowners here not only are threatened by a flood
of water but by a flood of tax lien foreclosures which would force
these people out of their homes."[53] Pointedly, Gonzalez reflected a
determination to protect small homeowners from unnecessary taxation.

---

[52]The Texas Observer, May 23, 1959, p. 2.

[53]San Antonio Light, March 4, 1959.

Among legislation that Gonzalez introduced was a bill to give teachers the right to participate in politics--a "Teachers' Bill of Rights." He also reintroduced a bill to establish a public defender system, and asked for legislation to protect union bargaining rights of bus drivers of the city-owned San Antonio Transit System. Elder aliens who had resided in Texas for more than twenty years would have been made eligible for old age assistance benefits under another bill submitted by Gonzalez. Veterans in urban areas would have benefitted from his bill authorizing loans for housing. But the 57th Legislature, according to one observer, confirmed "that government in Austin is by and for Monopoly."[54] (Reference here is to the major oil, gas, and utilities companies.) As a result, the "plain, common, ordinary run-of-the-mill citizen" was lost "in the shuffle"[55] and Gonzalez' bills did not become law.

On issues of major state-wide consequence, Gonzalez was most effective in his familiar role as a constructive irritant. He filibustered over four hours in protest to a bill changing the dates of primary elections from summer to spring. The bill was believed to be aimed at helping Senator Lyndon Johnson in his bid for the presidential nomination. In effect, the bill allowed Johnson to run for the Senate in May and not in July during the Democratic Convention. However, there were several items in the bill that would have produced

---

[54]The Texas Observer, July 25, 1959, p. 6.

[55]"Gonzalez for Governor" brochure, op. cit.

confusion and conflicts in the election process. Although Gonzalez was not thoroughly familiar with the bill, since no senator had been given time to read it, he predicted impending difficulties if the bill passed without study. The bill passed, but the governor threatened to veto it when he discovered the conflicting and confusing sections in it. Gonzalez was given credit with being "either the smartest or the luckiest politician in a long time" because of his prediction.[56] The bill was later corrected and signed into law.

Gonzalez also protested two bills by Senator William Fly of Victoria, the heir-apparent to Lieutenant Governor Ramsey, an avowed conservative. One of the bills was to permit raising of college student activities fees and the other was to reorganize the insurance commission. On the first, Gonzalez filibustered, arguing that the bill was a tax on those who could afford it least, and on the second, he accused Fly of conducting a personal vendetta against the insurance commissioner. Gonzalez also fought for passage of Governor Daniel's tax bill as opposed to a Senate substitute which excluded tax on natural gas and utilities companies.

When Senate colleagues of the conservative variety questioned Gonzalez' stand and suggested that he not be as verbal and critical, his answer was: "I wasn't elected to this office by any members of

---

[56]San Antonio Light, May 7, 1959.

the Senate. I was elected by the citizens of Bexar County, and they
are the only ones I owe anything to."[57]

There was little, if any, ground sacred to the established conservative hierarchy in Texas government that Gonzalez "feared to tread."
He thrived on the freewheeling tactics that Senate rules and custom
allowed him to pursue. Invitations to speak in all parts of the state
and in Colorado, California, Kansas, Michigan and other places kept
Gonzalez constantly on the move. Every day he would commute seventy-
two miles to Austin from his residence and return each night. He
reported to constituents via television in both Spanish and English.
All this plus his remarkable style led Paul Thompson to conclude that
Gonzalez' "colorful phrases, impish humor and deft jabs at the critical have endeared him to multitudes," and that if he was not stopped
in the next election "no telling how big he can grow or what bauble he
can snatch."[58]

One year before Gonzalez' term expired, Bexar Representative
R. L. "Bob" Strickland announced that he would run for the State
Senate. Strickland's announcement was premature, upsetting many of his
fellow conservatives who also considered running. As a result, before
the filing deadline, two more opponents threw their hats in the ring. One
was "Ozzie" Lattimer who Gonzalez had defeated in 1956 and the second was

---

[57] Jon Ford, "Gonzalez Breaking Sound Barrier," San Antonio
Express, July 16, 1959.

[58] Paul Thompson, "Top of the News," San Antonio News, July 8,
1959.

R. L. "Bob" Strickland, a businessman who coincidentally had the same
name as the state representative. Gonzalez announced for reelection,
charging that his election in 1956 had disturbed some people "who have
thrived on an undemocratic system" whereby the representatives are
"errand boys" for private interests instead of being "public ser-
vants."[59] Maury Maverick, Jr., the former legislator who had attributed
much of his success in 1950 to Gonzalez, remarked that the six conservative Bexar legislators treated the senator "with such white-hot hatred
in spots it had put him in a role he well knows how to play--that of
martyr."[60]

The 1960 primaries were charged with anticipation of the presidential election. Lyndon Johnson was going to bid for the Democratic
nomination and all Texans knew it. In Bexar County, liberals were
determined to defeat the Bexar Legislative Group of conservative representatives. For four years groups identified with the liberal wing of
the Democratic Party had been building up their forces. In 1960 a
coalition of labor, minority representatives, independent liberals,
and others, organized for a major effort in the primaries. A loose
coalition of candidates teamed up to run for the legislature and,
although Gonzalez was not an indigenous part of the group, no effort
was made to disassociate with them.

---

[59]San Antonio Light, May 24, 1959.

[60]Paul Thompson, "Top of the News," San Antonio News, July 8,
1959.

In an intensive and long campaign, Gonzalez asked for reelection with the slogan, "One good term deserves another." He pointed to his record in the Senate: the slum clearance law, the medical school bill, and his other legislative achievements. He campaigned against "special interests" that, he said, controlled the hands of his chief opponent, Representative Strickland. Strickland accused Gonzalez of irresponsibility, of being a headline hunter, and of being a lackey of Jimmy Hoffa and his "labor goons." Also raised was the question of Gonzalez' income, by now a well-worn issue.

The first primary balloting pushed Gonzalez into a run-off with Strickland. In the run-off Bexar County's conservative forces rallied to fight their last major legislative battle in the Democratic Party. Strickland conducted a well-financed, hard-hitting campaign against Gonzalez. The West Side and East Side were forfeited to Gonzalez as the major emphasis was on the North and South Sides. Again the tie-in with "Union Bosses" was attempted as Strickland published full page ads in newspapers warning voters of Gonzalez' union ties and pleading: "Don't Let Hoffa and Gonzalez Ruin our State."[61]

Strickland's campaign proved unsuccessful and Gonzalez was nominated handily. But he was forced to run again in the General Election against Ike Kampmann, a local attorney whose wife was a major officer of the State Republican Party. Gonzalez, however, did not devote as much time to his own campaign as he did to John Kennedy's.

---

[61]San Antonio News, June 1, 1960.

He campaigned in eleven states for Kennedy and the Democratic ticket
and was national Co-chairman of the Viva Kennedy Clubs.

Gonzalez had little difficulty in defeating Kampmann and even
ran ahead of Kennedy in Bexar County. Kennedy carried 91 precincts in
defeating Nixon by over 12,000 votes, whereas Gonzalez carried 121 precincts and defeated Kampmann by more than 18,000 votes. The election
assured Gonzalez of the position as the number one vote-getter among
local politicians. A number of conservative Democrats who had once
controlled party politics reneged at the Gonzalez, Kennedy, and coalition legislative victories and switched to the Republican Party.
Among these were R. L. "Bob" Strickland and Frates Seeligson.

Gonzalez' position as the leader of Bexar County legislators
strengthened his position in the Senate where his colleagues, including
arch foes such as Senator George Parkhouse of Dallas, seemed resigned
to the fact that Gonzalez was a member of the Senate and received him
graciously. In fact, Gonzalez teamed with Parkhouse to sponsor a
water bill deemed vital to future development of the state. But Gonzalez appeared restless in the Senate. The presidential campaign had
given him the opportunity to travel the country and meet congressional
and other national leaders and he had been well received by people
almost everywhere he went.

Kennedy's victory, of course, had elevated Lyndon Johnson to
the vice presidency. Johnson's Senate seat was to be filled by a
special election. Gonzalez' name was mentioned as a possible candidate, but so was Maverick's. The two men knew that if they both ran,

the liberal vote would be split, reducing the opportunity for either of them to win. However, in developments that proved almost permanently disastrous to liberals, both Gonzalez and Maverick ran for the United States Senate. Liberal and moderate forces divided and Republican John Tower and conservative Democrat William Blakely led the balloting.

There were a total of 71 candidates in the race and Gonzalez ran sixth, capturing a little less than 10 per cent of the total vote. However, the real victory for Gonzalez was in the outcome in Bexar County. The question of Gonzalez' local political strength was firmly settled as he finished first in the field of seventy-one. He ran far ahead of all Democratic candidates and polled 6,000 votes more than Republican Tower. The Light reported that "once again they [Bexar County voters] made it clear that State Senator Henry Gonzalez commands the largest and most loyal personal following of any local politician."[62]

Two months after the Senate election in which Gonzalez campaigned extensively for Democrat Blakely, President Kennedy announced the appointment of Bexar County Congressman Paul J. Kilday to the Court of Military Appeals. Gonzalez became the logical Democratic candidate to replace Kilday.

---

[62]San Antonio Light, April 5, 1961.

CHAPTER IV

EXPERIENCE COUNTS

On November 4, 1961, Henry Gonzalez was elected United States
Representative from the twentieth district of Texas. He had based his
campaign primarily on his prior training and experience. His literature emphasized that "in electing a U.S. Representative for Bexar
County experience and training count. . . . Henry Gonzalez has the
experience that makes him the trained man for you to send to Washington."[1] The leaflet then included biographical data that outlined the
seasoning he had undergone.

Henry Gonzalez is an unusual, perhaps unique, man. ("Perhaps
unique" is used because this writer is not prepared to deny the existence of other men like Gonzalez.) This same measure must be applied
to Gonzalez as a politician. The decision as to the uniqueness of
Gonzalez will be left to the reader. However, there are few men who
can boast of Gonzalez' cultural and intellectual development or of his
political training.

As a politician Gonzalez is "self-made" much like Carnegie and
Rockefeller were "self-made" millionaires. If he used any one formula
for success, it was, in his own words, "hard work." In explaining his

---

[1]"Experience Counts!" Campaign leaflet distributed by Gonzalez'
campaign headquarters.

victory in the congressional election, Gonzalez said: "It's important to get out and meet voters and work hard at it for years because you can't stereotype or pigeonhole humans, much as political leaders might like to."[2] Gonzalez' refusal to stereotype people is probably the second major factor in his success. To him each person is an individual who has motives, drives, views, and ideals all his own. Gonzalez acknowledges and respects these individual characteristics and the people sense this.

This writer once had the occasion to hear a local candidate remark that, by looking at a person's occupation and place of residence on the eligible voters list, he could tell whether the individual was a conservative or liberal,Democrat or Republican. Fortunately, the candidate was victorious in his campaign. Yet, in the final analysis, this "pigeonholing" could foreseeably force this man to retire from office after the next campaign. Gonzalez does not "write-off" the North Side in a political campaign just as he does not take the West Side for granted. Again, this brings the discussion back to the question of hard work, as this is the alternative to a refusal to stereotype.

As a city councilman, Gonzalez probably devoted more time to the duties of the office than any man since the adoption of council-manager government. On the council he developed and matured a practice which he has used every since. This was the methodical and

---

[2]Paul Thompson, San Antonio News, November 14, 1961.

thorough study of legislative proposals on which he had to vote. He
was determined to learn not only the proposals included in the legislation but their possible ramifications as well. This is why he often
raised a lonely voice in council or Senate meetings--he was often the
only member informed of all the provisions and their possible conse-
quences. Constituents noticed this trait in Gonzalez and therefore
voted for him. This writer is familiar with many citizens who acknowledge that they did not vote for Gonzalez when he first ran for office
but do so now because he carefully considers each measure before voting.

Diligence and hard work are necessary to continue close scru-
tiny of legislative proposals. Besides offering the officeholder self-
satisfaction, these traits reward him at the all-important ballot box.
In addition, the politician gains information and knowledge that will
probably help him in analyzing future legislation. Gonzalez sees the
value of this and his record reflects it. There were many instances
on the city council and in the Senate where Gonzalez called upon his
prior experiences and knowledge to clarify or explain a legislative
proposal.

Gonzalez has developed as few politicians have. He is well-
aware of the inner workings of a county courthouse. His years as a
juvenile officer provided him with the opportunity to know the problems of a law enforcement officer, to grasp the intricacies of courthouse politics, and to learn the social and cultural conditions that
contribute to juvenile delinquency. Later, with the Housing Authority,
he became well-acquainted with the difficulties experienced by

families in substandard housing. Besides providing him with experience, his work in these positions cultivated future votes. A retired
schoolteacher has expressed admiration for Gonzalez and has indicated
her consistent support for him in his campaigns. Her reasoning is
based on her observations of him as a juvenile officer: "Mr. Gonzalez
could talk to a young boy or girl who was not going to school and convince him to return to school. He did this when others were not able
to communicate with the child. Many boys and girls stayed in school
because of him."[3]

Gonzalez did not gain all his experience through work in the
juvenile office, with SAHA, or in the city council and in the State
Senate. His campaign biographies do not exaggerate when they read
that he has a "thirst for knowledge that is apparent everywhere he
goes" and that he is "well acquainted with writings of the Western
World's great philosophers, historians, and biographers."[4] A personal
library of approximately 6,000 volumes confirms this fact.

The books span a horizon of subjects from higher mathematics
to simple fiction and from space science to higher philosophy. He
still continues the prodigious reading habit which he began as a young
boy. He is an avid reader, always in the process of reading several
periodicals and books at one stage. No matter how late at night he
goes to bed, he reads before going to sleep. There is little that

---

[3] Interview with retired schoolteacher, April 24, 1965.

[4] Mimeographed campaign biography, 1961.

comes up in his official duties that he cannot trace or find parallel with his readings. Thus, a constant intellectual curiosity affords him the rewards of knowing the thoughts and experiences of others and allows him to apply them to his official duties.

As a man thoroughly devoted to public affairs, Gonzalez eats, sleeps, and drinks politics. He is honest and is concerned with the public welfare; he is devoted to public life often at the expense of family; and he is as open-minded as any man can be, for he avoids prejudging issues, events, and people unless he has a thorough knowledge of the particulars. However, these are traits that often are not publicly exhibited, and therefore, must be accepted as this writer's observations.

Gonzalez is idealistic, yet he is practical. He is idealistic enough to believe that the public good must come before special interest, and practical enough to know that often these issues are clouded and the best possible solution is sometimes a combination of both. He knows that the mores of an honest businessman cannot be equated to the mores of an honest politician. Thus, while he does not often criticize unscrupulous businessmen, he is quick to condemn their political counterparts. He holds sacred the position of public trust voters have entrusted him with, and questions business opportunities presented to him because he feels that they can be attributed to this political position rather than to shrewd investment.

Since his experience with the San Antonians on the city council, Gonzalez has shied from attachments to groups or factions for

campaign purposes. He himself has said: "I have to run as an independent, because that's the way I'm built; tickets are not good for the
general public."[5] Gonzalez' reasoning is that without close attachments he can carry out his plans as he sees fit and can explain why
he did or didn't do something. Personal decisions are the direct
responsibility of one man and Gonzalez functions best as one man. He
accepts mutual assistance agreements with others, but nothing that will
diffuse his personal responsibility. This discussion, however, must
be limited within the confines of the Democratic Party, for Gonzalez
is a strict party man.

This unwillingness to relinquish campaign authority to individuals or groups has caused some supporters to become disenchanted
with Gonzalez. The fact that he is not an organization man and does
not use campaign managers has dismayed more than one supporter, especially in his state-wide campaigns. Even in the 1961 congressional
campaign when an organized and united front of Democrats was a major
factor in his victory, Gonzalez campaigned somewhat independently.
Most organizational operations were conducted from Democratic Headquarters, but Gonzalez' speeches and schedules were products of his
personal headquarters in the Houston Building.

Gonzalez' popularity with voters is personal. His hard work
and relentless drive are surely major factors, but above this he has

---

[5]Jon Ford, "Gonzalez Rules Out Ticket With Spears," San
Antonio Express, June 7, 1959.

a magnetic personality that attracts people wherever he goes. His exploits as a filibusterer and orator and his natty dress, no doubt, lend color to his public image that makes him a campaigner par excellance.

His effect on Bexar County politics is remarkable. Probably more than any one man he revolutionized politics in Bexar County. As the first major Latin-American candidate for the legislature, he startled political observers by almost winning in 1950. At that time Latin Americans as a group were not as politically-oriented as they are now and they had minor effect on the decisions of local politicians. A year after his near victory, a Latin American was elected to the city council. Two years later Gonzalez was elected to the council and ever since there has been at least one Latin American on the city council.

During his tenure on the council, Gonzalez pushed, prodded, threatened, and pleaded with colleagues to take definite progressive action to correct the conditions mentioned in Chapter I. It is true that he was not alone and that he registered the sentiments of many citizens, but the point is that it was he who successfully prevented passage of unreasonable water and telephone rate hikes, and it was he who predicted a budgetary surplus when the city manager wouldn't or couldn't, and it was he who offered the desegregation ordinances. All of these actions were sort of minor revolutions within themselves against the established order. And if he did nothing else, he made city officials "think," as several of them admitted.

No contemporary can precisely measure the impact Gonzalez had in the State Senate as the first Latin American to be elected to that body. The filibusters against segregation removed the blocks from the train of progress which otherwise might have been delayed indefinitely. Had the segregation bills passed without resistence, it is likely that a flood of reactionary legislation would have washed away the bridge to the twentieth century in Texas.

His segregation filibusters were not isolated accomplishments. For Gonzalez' voice was constantly raised in the Senate as the voice of a devil's advocate--a constructive irritant. He played a role in the State Senate not unlike that of the Loyal Opposition of British Parliament. It must be noted that only in the Senate can this role be played best, for there the rules and customs allow a filibuster or at least a prolonged debate. In a state that, in matters of progressive legislation, is generations behind California and Wisconsin, Gonzalez constantly reminded his colleagues and the people of the problems Texas must face as a consequence. Because of this role Gonzalez has sometimes been called quixotic. In a sense, this title is not completely erroneous, for Gonzalez is an admirer of Cervantes' gift of poignant satire.

Gonzalez' skill as a legislator can be measured by noting that in five years in the Senate he handled, co-sponsored, or introduced forty-two bills that became law. Of these, he personally is proudest of the urban renewal law which passed the Senate after receiving an unfavorable committee report, and passage of the medical school bill

in the Senate by a vote of twenty-five to four over the active opposition of some influential senators. It is not unreasonable to say that
he was a powerful state senator for he could hold the Senate at bay
with merely the threat of a filibuster. His filibuster record shows
that his talkathons were not futile, for they often delayed hasty
action, provided key amendments, or killed whole sections, and they
usually directed public attention to the issues.

In his 1960 campaign for reelection to the Senate, Gonzalez
was accused of having poor relationships with colleagues because he
was often extremely critical of many of them. This, however, must be
considered an inaccurate statement produced by the heat of a campaign.
Gonzalez has always been aware of the vital need of maintaining rapport with colleagues and he has been extremely successful in doing so.
However, this rapport has been based on a mutual respect for each individual's principles and convictions, rather than in superficial nice-
ties that evade the issues and avoid the truth. Gonzalez can best be
described (to use well-known but accurate clichés) as one who believes
in pulling no punches and in speaking straight from the shoulder.
But his colleagues, though sometimes taken aback by his statements,
respected him for his honesty and forthrightness.

The Secretary of the Senate, Charles Schnabel, is a man who,
by virtue of his position, intimately knows the members of the Senate.
He is and must be a close observer of the moods and actions of the
Senate. Thus, Schnabel must be considered qualified to comment on Gonzalez' relations with other senators. Schnabel does not hesitate to
state that Gonzalez was well-liked and accepted by his colleagues.

It must be remembered that Gonzalez entered the Senate with two handicaps: He was the first Latin American elected to that body and was considered by some as "that Mexican," and he was known as an outspoken liberal--an unwelcomed attribute in the conservative Texas Senate. However, Schnabel believes that Gonzalez quickly overcame these handicaps for two reasons: First, his keen intelligence allowed him to demonstrate vast knowledge of history, literature, and politics, and to interpret the scope and effect of legislative proposals; and secondly, his personality allowed him to get along with people even though they were political opponents. Schnabel points out that Gonzalez possesses an outgoing, effervescent personality and he enjoys meeting and talking with people who, in turn, enjoy meeting and talking with him.[6]

Senator William N. Patman, son of U.S. Representative Wright Patman who is Dean of the Texas delegation, sent Gonzalez a letter that captured the essence of Texas Senate opinion about him and provided a penetrating analysis of his Senate accomplishments. The letter said, in part:

> While I have admired your being a gentleman in the noblest sense of the word, I have also been a great admirer of your toughness-- a toughness grounded in high principle, nurtured by a deep sympathy for the problems of all mankind, and activated by an enthusiastic desire to do the right thing. But no matter how urgent the cause you pleaded, you never marred your conduct by petty discourtesies, arrogant sarcasm, or mean misbehavior. I have seen you on countless occasions stand up as a true advocate for what

---

[6]Interview with Charles Schnabel, Secretary of the Senate, Austin, Texas, November 23, 1964.

you knew to be right. It always seemed rather that your convictions fed upon adversity, that your character strengthened upon opposition, and your eloquence flowered by exposure to the most trying circumstances. Your magnificent sense of humor turns a carping criticism into a joke on the offender. Your dauntless courage permits no shadow of fear.[7]

Perhaps the most significant testimony to the regard and esteem that colleagues held for Gonzalez is in the unanimous resolution passed by the Senate memorializing Congress of the Senate's pride in Gonzalez' service to the state. No other state senator who has moved up to the Congress, and there have been several, has received such a tribute. This resolution was inserted in the Congressional Record by Senator Ralph Yarborough and Representative Wright Patman.[8]

The demands on a congressman to assist constituents are well known, and Gonzalez was prepared to meet these demands. As councilman and senator he devoted much of his time to the interests of individual constituents. He always maintained an office in the Houston Building in downtown San Antonio. In letters to constituents, in radiobroadcasts, and in television reports Gonzalez emphasized his availability to consult with constituents and invited them to his office. But his contacts with constituents were not limited to office visits, for everywhere he went he was approached by troubled citizens who requested advice or assistance, and he always tried to comply.

---

[7]William Patman to Henry B. Gonzalez, September 18, 1961, Gonzalez' Senate letters file.

[8]U.S., Congressional Record, (reprints) 87th Cong., 2d Sess., 1962.

There probably has never been a legislative official in Bexar
County who has been as readily available and as willing to consult and
assist constituents as has Gonzalez. There are several factors that
point to this conclusion. Before Gonzalez' emergence into politics,
Latin Americans were generally distrustful of officeholders and consequently did not attempt to seek their assistance. Those who did seek
assistance were often ignored unless they had intermediaries to insure
that they would be heard. However, Gonzalez went out of his way to
assist everyone who asked. He developed no screening policy and thus
saw personally as many people as he could. It became common to over-
hear neighbors advise one another: "Why don't you go see Gonzalez,
he'll try to help you."

Gonzalez, of course, did not limit his availability to Latin
Americans. In fact, he cultivated Anglos' confidence in his ability
by continually assisting those who sought his help. Also, his public
stands against book burning, utilities rates increases, the sales tax,
and general sympathy for the underdog prompted many Anglos to seek him
out whenever they found themselves in need of assistance or advice.
One long-time supporter said, "Henry Gonzalez is the most sincere politician I have ever known of; he honestly attempts to carry out and do
everything he promises."[9]

Thus, the population of Bexar County developed a confidence
that they could "fight city hall" if they went to Gonzalez. And he

---

[9]Interview with Gonzalez supporter, February 10, 1965.

was not encumbered by potential conflict of interest due to a business
or professional stake in the citizens' requests. He was not a practicing
attorney and therefore could not accept the citizens as potential clients;
he did not invest in commercial ventures and therefore could not be placed
in a position of a conflict of interest when he attempted to help constituents. In other words, Gonzalez was free to assist constituents
solely on the merits of their cause and not on special or private considerations. As a politician, Gonzalez realized the value of this
conflict-free position and used it to cultivate the confidence of
voters. It is certain that he was successful in doing so.

While in the Senate, Gonzalez became known throughout the state for
his views and his achievements. The campaigns for governor and U. S.
senator gave him further opportunity to travel and to meet people
in all sections of Texas. Gonzalez' influence also carried to other
states, primarily through Latin Americans living in these areas. In
California, he inspired the formation of Henry B. Gonzalez Democratic
Clubs in 1958. He addressed the national conventions of the American
GI Forum and the League of United Latin American Citizens first in 1954
when he was on the city council and continued to do so as state
senator. Gonzalez became the voice of the Latin-American minority
in this country. He assured them that "my own career is an illustration that the walls of prejudice can crumble." because "you will
be heard when you have something to offer."[10]

---

[10]
Henry B. Gonzalez, speech to National Convention Banquet,
American GI Forum, Albuquerque, New Mexico, August 24, 1957, from "Pro-
ceedings of National Convention, 1957."

John Kennedy believed that Gonzalez had "something to offer" and asked him to organize Viva Kennedy Clubs throughout the nation during the 1960 presidential campaign. Gonzalez served as national co-chairman of the organization with U.S. Senator Dennis Chavez of New Mexico. The organization is credited as having played a critical part in the Kennedy victory.

The Kennedy-Gonzalez relationship is in itself worthy of special attention. The two first met in 1951 when Gonzalez attended the National Convention on Housing in Washington as a delegate of the Alamo Chapter of the National Organization of the Housing Officials. Kennedy was then a congressman and was one of the convention speakers. Gonzalez met Kennedy briefly, and he says that he was impressed by the congressman's knowledge of the facts, and interests in housing problems, yet, he "looked like a kid."

The two did not meet again until 1956 when Kennedy, by then a senator, made a campaign address for Adlai Stevenson in San Antonio. Gonzalez, then Democratic nominee for state senator, reminded Kennedy of the first meeting. Kennedy recalled the convention and, according to Gonzalez, they exchanged letters regularly after 1956. In 1957 Kennedy requested Gonzalez to help the son of a constituent who was at Lackland Air Force Base in San Antonio. In 1959 Robert Kennedy, who was in Austin for a speech at The University of Texas, conferred with Gonzalez about Senator Kennedy's campaign opportunities in Texas. Gonzalez advised him that, because Lyndon Johnson would be a native-son candidate at the Democratic Convention, Kennedy would do better concentrating on delegates from other states.

Gonzalez campaigned in eleven states and conferred with Kennedy twice during the campaign. He also toured Texas with Robert Kennedy. The Sunday before the Inauguration Gonzalez received a personal call from President-elect Kennedy who offered to appoint Gonzalez ambassador to a Latin-American country. The country was unspecified and was to have been determined after consultation with Dean Rusk, forthcoming Secretary of State. Gonzalez was overwhelmed by the offer, but did not hesitate in refusing it. He confided to Kennedy that he preferred to campaign for the U.S. Senate, and, if he lost, to serve out his term as state senator. He said that his ambitions were in the legislative field, not in diplomatic circles.[11]

The appointment of Representative Paul J. Kilday to the Court of Military Appeals provided Gonzalez with the opportunity to pursue his ambitions in the legislative field. Gonzalez was the acknowledged top vote-getter in San Antonio. He had campaigned for office seven times in Bexar County since 1950. His knowledge of the moods, interests, and needs of the people in the county was enhanced with each of these elections. Except for the run-off loss in 1950 and the 1958 loss to Governor Price Daniel, Gonzalez carried Bexar County in all of his campaigns and steadily increased his vote totals.

A coalition of conservative Democrats and Republicans was unable to defeat him in 1956 and 1960. His campaign experience, hard

---

[11]Henry B. Gonzalez, in address to meeting of Incarnate Word College Young Democrats, December 15, 1964.

work, and devotion to duty had earned him the opportunity to be the
major contender for the congressional seat.

In 1961 Gonzalez was the best known politician in San Antonio.
He and his supporters felt that he was the best qualified Democrat for
Congress. His fame as an orator, a champion of the people, and a dedicated public official was established. As friend and adviser to President Kennedy and Vice-President Johnson he held an unofficial position
of national confidence. There was no question as to his legislative
experience. Gonzalez had grown in stature since 1950 and now felt the
need to expand his official sphere of influence. The congressional
campaign provided him with the opportunity to move up in the legislative field--his chosen profession. The results indicate that the
voters agreed with him that experience counts.

The campaign itself provided a dramatic setting for Gonzalez'
ascendence to national political office. As the first congressional
campaign since Kennedy's election, it was depicted as the initial test
of the President's New Frontier program. _Time_ and the _Washington Post_
and other major periodicals and newspapers closely followed campaign
developments. Nationwide audiences viewed campaign highlights on net-
work television news programs. Both political parties sent funds,
advice, and personnel from their state and national headquarters in
extensive efforts to influence the outcome. The nation's eyes and
ears were trained on San Antonio, especially in the latter part of the
campaign.

Gonzalez' major opponent was John Goode, a lawyer, who had resigned his position as Republican County Chairman to make the race. Goode was a veteran of Republican Party battles and had served as county chairman for five years. In contrast to Gonzalez, Goode considered himself a conservative Republican. Although he had never before campaigned for public office, his behind-the-scenes work as party chairman provided him with great political experience. He was not publicly well known, but most politically-oriented businessmen knew him well. He was a combat veteran of the Marine Corps and had received several battle decorations.

Although the nation viewed the campaign as a battleground for acceptance of the Kennedy program, Republicans were not anxious to vigorously challenge the New Frontier in an area that had given the President a sizable victory just one year before. Goode decided to concentrate on the importance of local military installations to San Antonio's economic well-being. He reasoned that because of the city's dependence on military spending it was necessary that the local congressman be a member of the Armed Services Committee. (Kilday had served on the Armed Services Committee for sixteen years.)

Since the Democrats had filled the committee vacancy soon after Kilday's resignation, Goode maintained Gonzalez would not be given a seat on the committee. On the other hand, Goode said that he had been promised a seat by his party leaders. Thus, Goode campaigned as the only candidate who could become a member of the Armed Services

Committee, and, therefore, the only candidate who could adequately protect the military installations, the city's major industry.

In addition, a review of Republican campaign tactics, as reflected in newspaper coverage, reveals that Goode seldom criticized Kennedy's policies and often omitted the Republican label in advertisements. Gonzalez was depicted as a perennial office seeker who was a member of the Americans for Democratic Action (ADA). The organization was described by Republicans as a radical left-wing group denounced even by President Kennedy and an advocate of granting diplomatic recognition to Red China. Gonzalez' failure to be a lawyer also diminished his qualifications for Congress, according to Republicans, since "a lawyer has the advantage of knowing law."[12]

As the Democratic candidate, Gonzalez said he would push for the New Frontier, and he emphasized his personal friendship with Kennedy. Republican logic concerning the Armed Services Committee was countered by reasoning that committee membership was relatively valueless without majority party status, and the Democrats controlled the House, the Senate, and the Administration. However, Gonzalez' main theme was his legislative experience. As the "only candidate with a successful law-making history," Gonzalez said he would be able to "pay

---

[12]Paid political advertisement for John Goode, San Antonio News, October 26, 1961.

attention to the thousands of individual problems" and not be forced
to "spend his time trying to find his way around."[13]

Both parties sent some of their top personalities into Bexar
County on behalf of their respective candidates. The Republicans sent
former President Dwight Eisenhower. The visit was like a homecoming
to Eisenhower who had been stationed at Fort Sam Houston, coached high
school and college football, and married his wife, Mamie, in San
Antonio. It was a triumphant visit for the former President and it
probably marked the peak of Goode's campaign.

However, the Democrats were the party in power and therefore
had an arsenal of political power to unleash. Representative Carl
Albert, acting majority leader from Oklahoma, spoke at a testimonial
dinner for Gonzalez which was attended by Mrs. Lyndon Johnson and eight
of Gonzalez' State Senate colleagues. Endorsements came in from Governor Price Daniel, the Texas House delegation, Senator Ralph Yarborough,
and President John Kennedy. On the final days of the campaign, Vice-
President Lyndon Johnson and a caravan of aides arrived in San Antonio
to campaign for Gonzalez.

Extensive organizational efforts were combined by both parties.
Thousands of volunteers manned telephones, distributed material, and
did block canvassing. Bexar County Republicans had maintained a reputation for organizational work, but the Democratic Coalition matched

---

[13]Paid political advertisement for Henry B. Gonzalez, San
Antonio News, October 24, 1961.

Republican efforts. Every corner of the county was covered by the candidates or their campaign volunteers.

Election results show that the campaign stimulated more interest than any other special election in Bexar County history. Over 90,000 votes were cast, more than in any similar election. Every area of the city produced a turnout of over 60 per cent of its eligible voters. On the West Side 75 per cent of the voters turned out and gave Gonzalez a margin of over 12,000 votes. Goode's strongholds in the "silk-stocking" areas produced 6 to 1 majorities for the Republican candidate, but they were no match for Gonzalez' 12 to 1 margins on the West Side and 9 to 1 on the East Side. Final tabulations indicate that Gonzalez won by more than 10,000 votes.[14]

The campaign and the election result illustrated that Gonzalez' mastery at uniting the "potent combination" of minorities and attracting a sizable number of Anglo voters made him the number one politician in Bexar County and congressman from the twentieth district of Texas. Indeed experience counts.

---

[14]San Antonio Light, November 5, 1961.

CHAPTER V

THE CONGRESSMAN FROM BEXAR

A leading newspaper said that Henry B. Gonzalez' election to
the United States House of Representatives was "good not only for San
Antonio but for the country."[1] It is certain that in the period he
has been a congressman, Gonzalez has worked diligently to live up to
these editorial comments. Yet, the knowledge that much was expected
of him, coupled with the realization that as a congressman he has a
twofold responsibility of protecting San Antonio's interests and influ-
encing the national will, caused Gonzalez to question his own abili-
ties. He was humbled by the magnitude of his job and of his
responsibilities.

In many respects a vast gulf exists between the Legislature of
Texas and Congress. As a careful student of history and government,
Gonzalez was aware of this gulf and unsure that he could span it. In
the State Senate issues were often clouded by personalities, and personal or special interest motives were sometimes the deciding factor
in producing legislation. Gonzalez realized that in the Congress
decisions had to be made in the national interest based on a discussion
of the issues, not personalities. This had to be the procedure because
the stakes were too high. Could he meet the test?

---

[1] *Washington Post*, November 12, 1962.

Although this discussion may appear trivial, it is certain
that Gonzalez was deeply affected by the sudden realization that he
was, indeed, a congressman. Gonzalez' reactions can be compared somewhat to those a new President experiences when he assumes office. No
matter how much he has prepared himself for the job, no matter how
much he knows about its responsibilities, a new President undergoes a
sobering and humbling experience when he assumes the burdens and
powers of office. In a sense, Gonzalez was similarly affected when he
assumed his congressional office. And, as in the case of the President, the success of a congressman's tenure depends on how he measures
up to the responsibilities of office.

A congressman must perform several roles in order to serve
effectively. Basically, his duties are divided into those involving
legislation and those dealing with his constituency. Constitutionally,
his duties as a legislator are paramount; however, he is often forced
to devote most of his time and energies to problems of his district
and its residents. Also, because of certain political, social, and
personal circumstances, a congressman is required to perform other
roles. Gonzalez accepted the responsibility and assumed these roles.

As a Democrat, Gonzalez has certain party responsibilities; he
also has responsibilities as a supporter of the Democratic administrations which have been in power since his election. Another role Gonzalez has assumed is that of watchdog over federal agencies, particularly the Federal Aviation Agency. As a member of the House, he has
the responsibility of educating and informing the public of facts and

situations they would not know otherwise. Finally, as a politician,
he must submit himself to the voters for reelection. These roles cannot be completely isolated from each other, for they are often interrelated and overlapping. It is believed, however, that by treating
these roles separately, a more penetrating analysis can be made of
Gonzalez as a United States Representative.

Gonzalez went to Washington with most of his constituents
hoping he would be appointed to the Armed Services Committee. Throughout the campaign, Republicans had continuously emphasized the importance of having Bexar County's congressman on this committee. Since
Gonzalez' predecessor, Paul Kilday, served on the committee for over
twenty years, local citizens felt Gonzalez was entitled to the appointment. Also, it was believed that, without having its congressman on
the committee, the district might lose some of its military installations. Thus, in a very real sense, Gonzalez' committee assignment was
his first major crisis in office.

The leadership of Congress was aware of Gonzalez' problem and
Speaker John McCormack offered to push for enlargement of the Armed
Services Committee so that Gonzalez could be selected. But he warned
that such a move could antagonize some colleagues who also wanted a
place on the committee. The Speaker stated, however, that, if Gonzalez felt the committee assignment was crucial and was needed to
insure his reelection, an effort would be made to secure the position
for him.

Gonzalez was faced with a dilemma: should he reject the Speaker's offer and possibly jeopardize his reelection or should he accept the offer and risk antagonizing certain colleagues, especially members of the Texas delegation which operated under the seniority rule? Gonzalez advised Speaker McCormack that he did not want a special effort made to place him on the Armed Services Committee; he said that he would follow the customary rules and procedures of the House. He added that he did not believe voters would turn against him for failure to gain a seat on the Armed Services Committee.

Instead, Gonzalez was assigned to the Committee on Banking and Currency. He requested this assignment because its area of jurisdiction concerned matters in which he had specific interest and experience. The committee has a wide latitude of jurisdiction from banking and international finance to public housing and price controls. He had served on the Banking Committee in the State Senate and he had experience and interest in urban renewal, public housing, and consumer problems. He realized that a congressman's most productive legislative work is in the areas in which he felt most competent.

At first Gonzalez was disappointed with the committee's inactivity. The chairman was an octogenarian from the South who seldom convened the group. Gonzalez became a close friend of Representative Wright Patman of Texarkana, Texas, who was also an activist. Both men felt the committee was failing in its duty to fully investigate the feasibility of pending legislation within its jurisdiction. When the committee sent two bills concerning the Federal Reserve System to the floor, Gonzalez and Patman joined in dissent. They maintained that proper hearings had not been conducted and that the bills were privileged legislation for the Federal Reserve Banks.

The first bill, H.R. 8874, authorized certain banks to invest in corporations which provide clerical services for them. Gonzalez and Patman argued: "The bill raised serious problems under the antitrust laws, and may open the door to restraints of trade, price fixing, and bank mergers." Then, when the House was asked to consider legislation which gave the Federal Reserve System an additional $30,000,000 to build new branch banks, the representatives called the action "backdoor spending at its worst," and said, "It involves an abdication of congressional responsibility over the spending of public funds."[2]

However, committee work did not consume much of Gonzalez' time in 1962. But in 1963 Patman became chairman of the committee and reorganized and rejuvenated it. He was anxious to move into detailed studies in such areas as banking, the Federal Reserve System, and housing. Gonzalez was assigned to subcommittees on bank supervision and insurance, consumer affairs, and housing and thus was able to work in his areas of deep interest.

In the 88th Congress, approximately fourteen bills of major significance which were handled by the Banking and Currency Committee became law. Among these were the Urban Mass Transportation Act and the Housing Act of 1964. Gonzalez worked diligently in the hearings

---

[2]U.S. Congressional Record, August 14, 1962, pp. 15467, 15469.

and work sessions. The Housing Act had been considered one of the
most important legislative proposals of the New Frontier and Great
Society programs and, as a member of the subcommittee that authored
it, he played a key role in its passage. His work was acknowledged by
an invitation to the White House to witness President Johnson sign the
act into law.

In an effort to capitalize on Gonzalez' fluency in Spanish and
his interest in Latin-American affairs, committee chairman Patman
appointed him special liaison representative on Latin-American affairs
for the Banking and Currency Committee. In this capacity, Gonzalez
attended a conference of the Inter-American Development Bank Board of
Directors in Panama in April, 1964. At the beginning of the 89th Congress in January, 1965, Patman named Gonzalez to the subcommittee on
international finance with instructions to specialize in Latin-American
finance.

Gonzalez is gradually building seniority as he is now third
ranking member on the housing subcommittee, fourth ranking in international finance, and fifth ranking in consumer affairs. His overall
effectiveness and productivity will depend, of course, on his seniority
and his special talents. However, the devotion to committee work and
careful study of legislative measures which marked his early career,
has, if anything, been intensified during his tenure as a congressman.

Although the Banking and Currency Committee enjoys wide latitude in its jurisdiction, there are multitudes of legislative measures
that Gonzalez is asked to judge that are not within the scope of the

committee. Many are of extreme importance such as the Economic Opportunities Act and the Social Security Amendments Act of 1965. Gonzalez
has been persistent in his efforts to listen carefully during debate
on key issues. Some individuals who know of Gonzalez' reputation as a
filibusterer find it difficult to believe that he is a careful listener
too. However, the rules and customs of the House do not lend themselves to unlimited debate and Gonzalez, more often than not, just fol-
lows the debate. He usually studies the reports and evidence which
accompany the bills to the floor. This information is provided to
help House members understand the bills; Gonzalez often collects the
discarded material after adjournment and sends it to constituents with
an interest in the particular measure.

Gonzalez has been active in introducing about thirty public
bills and eight resolutions. In the 88th Congress, nine of the bills
and two resolutions were incorporated in acts that became law. Three
of the bills were incorporated into the Economic Opportunities Act of
1964. One authorized the establishment of a youth conservation corps
and resulted in the job corps section of the anti-poverty law; another
authorized the establishment of a national service corps similar to
the Volunteer in Service to America (VISTA) program; and the last provided for instruction of illiterate adults, a program also authorized
under the anti-poverty law.

The Library Services Act of 1964 incorporated his bill to
improve public and school library facilities; a bill authorizing Texas
to obtain Social Security coverage for policemen was incorporated into

Public Law 88-350; and a bill to establish a commission to study settlement of the political status of Puerto Rico was incorporated into Public Law 88-271. The Dual Compensation Act of 1964 incorporated his bill to exempt certain reserve officers and non-regular members of the armed services from the law. He was the first congressman to introduce a bill, which was incorporated into Public Law 88-256, authorizing the coinage of fifty-cent pieces commemorating the late President John F. Kennedy. The law authorizing the President to offer Winston Churchill honorary United States citizenship was similar to a Gonzalez measure first introduced in 1962. Public Law 88-242 authorizing the President to designate the first week in March as "Save Your Vision Week" was similar to a resolution Gonzalez introduced in September, 1963.

One of the most difficult tasks for a House member is to stay informed of the details and intricacies of legislative measures. Gonzalez' custom of carefully reading details of legislation allows him to be well-informed, but he still uses additional aides to help in the task. He makes frequent use of committee reports and hearings, his legislative assistant often makes special briefs for him, and the Legislative Reference Service of the Library of Congress provides special information when needed. Another source of information are letters from constituents and discussions with San Antonians when he returns to the district on weekends. In addition, he is a member of the Democratic Study Group, a group of liberal congressmen, and, as a member, is furnished with special information on legislation. Of course, lucrative sources of knowledge are his colleagues who serve on the other committees.

Since most legislative measures are not products of a congressman's committee, usually he can register his opinion only at voting time. Some congressmen, no doubt, are anxious not to register their vote in order to avoid possible repercussions at home. However, Gonzalez, throughout his career, has always attempted to vote on every issue before him. From 1962 to 1964 there were 806 quorum calls and roll call votes in the House, and Gonzalez was present for 99 per cent of them.[3] Gonzalez says that one of his primary objectives as an officeholder is to cast a vote on each issue so that the public can know where he stands.[4]

At times Gonzalez has taken positions on controversial issues that have resulted in considerable publicity. One of these was his vote in 1963 against additional appropriations for the House Committee on Un-American Activities. According to Gonzalez, his vote was instigated primarily by the knowledge that the committee received the highest committee allowance and yet produced only three legislative measures in the period of its existence. Gonzalez made his decision to vote against appropriations for the committee after listening to Wright Patman bemoan the fact that the Banking and Currency Committee received less funds than the Un-American Activities Committee. His "no" vote

---

[3]San Antonio Light, September 20, 1964.

[4]Interview with Henry B. Gonzalez, December 18, 1964.

was only one of twenty and, because of it, he gained considerable
notoriety among right-wing and super-patriotic groups. In San Antonio,
The Johnathan Wainright American Legion Post called his vote a "dis-
graceful act" against the security of the country.[5]

A flurry of letters to the editors of local newspapers began
criticizing Gonzalez' stand. His main reason for voting against the
appropriations was his belief that the committee should not be given
more funds, but later investigation and study of the issue led him to
conclude that the committee's functions should be placed under the
jurisdiction of the Judiciary Committee. This was a proposal that
Representative James Roosevelt (Dem.-Calif.) has advocated for several
years. In the 89th Congress, Gonzalez voted for an unsuccessful
motion to send the question of the House Un-American Activities Committee's appropriation back to committee, but he did not vote against
the actual appropriation. When the issue of investigating the Ku Klux
Klan was raised, Gonzalez signed a statement with some twenty-five
colleagues opposing an investigation that would not provide the wit-
nesses with proper constitutional safeguards; later he voted against
additional appropriations for the committee to investigate the Ku Klux
Klan.

On civil rights Gonzalez has been as outspoken as he was on
the city council and in the State Senate. He considers civil rights
a moral issue and not one in which reasonable men can have honest

---

[5]Militant American, January, 1964.

differences. He voted for the Civil Rights Act of 1964 and said that it was legislation that should have been passed in the nineteenth century. The first bill he introduced after taking the oath of office in 1962 was a constitutional amendment to ban the poll tax requirements in all elections, national, state, and local. He then supported the proposal that passed the Congress outlawing poll tax requirements for voting in federal elections. Shortly after the church bombing in Birmingham, Alabama, in 1963, he obtained a special order from the Speaker to address the House on the civil rights issue. Twenty colleagues, both Democrats and Republicans joined him in the venture. In a letter to a lawyer from Birmingham who wrote to him about "keeping the blood stream pure," Gonzalez said: "Your arguments are not worthy of a lawyer. They would be worthy of a Hitler, for they stink."[6]

As a Democrat and as a political ally of both John Kennedy and Lyndon Johnson, Gonzalez has been a constant supporter of their administrations' measures such as the Housing Act and the Area Redevelopment Act. In fact, he cast the deciding vote for the Area Redevelopment Act in committee in 1965. On the floor of the House he has been one of the most loyal administration supporters. In 1964 the Congressional Quarterly compiled a record of votes and listed Gonzalez with a 96 per cent pro-administration rating.[7] He had the highest of any Texan.

---

[6] Henry B. Gonzalez to Birmingham Lawyer, May 22, 1964.

[7] Congressional Quarterly, October 30, 1964, p. 2601.

Gonzalez assured himself that President Johnson would be aware of this rating when he wrote to the President informing him of the fact.[8]

On domestic issues Gonzalez has been a strong supporter of the Democratic administrations. In fact, statements he made during his campaign that he was ahead of the New Frontier are probably true when one looks at civil rights and the anti-poverty program. Democratic budgetary policies have also received strong support from Gonzalez, particularly in his newsletters to constituents. Letters to constituents also show his support for the administration.

On foreign policy Gonzalez probably was more vociferous in support of Kennedy than he has been of Johnson. Gonzalez has been an outspoken advocate of the Alliance for Progress and has often inserted favorable reports in the Congressional Record. On the Cuban question, Gonzalez joined with six colleagues and offered the resolution which supported Kennedy's action in blockading Cuba and was called in on consultations during the crisis in 1965. He approved whole-heartedly the Nuclear Test Ban Treaty and had Ambassador Averell Harriman, the chief negotiator, on his television program.

With the Johnson administration his support of foreign policy has been somewhat qualified--if not publicly, at least privately. Although he voted for the resolution supporting Johnson's actions in the Gulf of Tonkin he had misgivings about his vote. He now marvels

---

[8]Henry B. Gonzalez to President Lyndon Johnson, November 20, 1965.

that only Adam Clayton Powell did not vote for the resolution--Powell voted "present." Again, he expressed misgivings when he voted for the $700,000,000 supplemental appropriations for Viet Nam. When Johnson sent troops to the Dominican Republic he assured his television report viewers that the President did what he had to, but privately he expressed doubts.[9]

Gonzalez' concern and interest in Latin America are prompted by his close cultural and social ties to the people of that area. He often meets with officials from Latin America visiting in Washington. The Voice of America frequently asks him to tape programs in Spanish, and he has made a special film in Spanish for the United States Information Service. Kennedy was and Johnson is aware of Gonzalez' potential in helping United States relations with Latin countries. Kennedy and Johnson invited him to White House receptions for leaders of Latin-American countries, and Johnson asked him to go to California and El Paso, Texas for meetings with the President of Mexico.

Gonzalez' close affinity to the Democratic Party is well known. He usually is a rigid party man and administration officials have asked him to give partisan speeches in most areas of the country. Gonzalez' many encounters with Republicans in Texas elections have embittered him somewhat against them. Since the election for state senator in 1956, they have opposed him consistently during and after campaigns. He is not resentful that Republicans oppose him, as he believes that

---

[9]Interview with Henry B. Gonzalez, April 2, 1965.

constructive opposition makes him a better politician. However, he
dislikes what he believes is an over-emphasis on personalities and
their distorting of facts in campaigns against him. He has little, if
any, use for local Republican leaders although he counts several Republican colleagues among his friends.

Gonzalez' devotion to the Democratic Party has been intensified by his observations that Republicans, such as Senator John Tower
and former Representative Bruce Alger, have been a tremendous handicap
for Texas in Congress and with the administration. Since they voted
consistently against Democratic measures, it is difficult for their
constituents to enlist their aid in attempts to participate in urban
renewal, public housing, or other programs which have been inspired by
the Democrats. On the other hand, Gonzalez has been loyal to Democratic programs. For example, in 1963 in 47 key votes he was rated 98
per cent for the second highest party unity score among Democrats in
the House.[10] Gonzalez supports the Democratic Party because he feels
its members believe that "the Party must serve, not profit or dominate."[11] Gonzalez believes that, whenever members of the Party or of
the administration attempt to profit or dominate, he has a duty to
inform the public of their actions.

---

[10]Congressional Quarterly Almanac, 88th Congress, XIX (Washington, D.C.: Congressional Quarterly Service, 1964), 733.

[11]Interview with Henry B. Gonzalez, November 3, 1965.

Although the President, through his cabinet, is responsible
for the actions of all administrative officers, there are some agencies
established by Congress which are independent and not responsible to
cabinet members. The actions of these independent agencies are further
isolated by the fact that often their areas of responsibility are
highly technical and beyond the comprehension of presidential aides or
congressional staffs. It is well known that some agency budget
requests are understood by few, if any, members of Congress. One of
these independent agencies is the Federal Aviation Agency (FAA), which
has jurisdiction over air traffic control and air safety standards.

After his election in 1960, President Kennedy appointed Najeeb
Halaby Administrator of the FAA. Halaby had raised considerable campaign funds for Kennedy in California and had been a member of the
Eisenhower-appointed advisory committee which had originally recom-
mended the establishment of the FAA. When Halaby assumed the position
he began to make several changes in the operations of the agency. In
1961, before Gonzalez arrived in Washington, Halaby announced the trans-
fer of the air route traffic control center from San Antonio to
Houston. The move, according to Halaby, was to insure air safety and
promote economy. The control center in New Orleans was also to be
consolidated with the one in Houston.

Gonzalez protested the move because the agency had not publicly
explained its claim that the move would bring about economy and air
safety. When Gonzalez requested information from the agency in support
of its announcement, Halaby was reluctant to comply. In addition,

Halaby, while in San Antonio, was caustic and rude with local civic leaders who questioned him on the proposed move. Also, he criticized Gonzalez for his protests, and referred to him as "a freshman congressman acting like a freshman." The new congressman needed little encouragement after that remark to continue his protests of the proposed move; nor was there need to prompt Gonzalez to become a severe critic of Halaby's role as an administrator.

In the months that followed Halaby's visit to San Antonio, Gonzalez criticized Halaby repeatedly on the floor of the House and in insertions in the Congressional Record. In the period from August 6, 1962, to August 17, 1962, Gonzalez' criticisms of Halaby appeared in the Record on ten separate occasions.[12] In answer to Halaby's remark about Gonzalez' lack of seniority, the congressman said:

> Mr. Halaby is right about my being a freshman congressman. In fact, I am so much a "freshman" that I still think that the head of a public agency is a public servant, and as a servant he must account for his actions and decisions. I am so much a "freshman" that I still dislike arrogance and rudeness on the part of public servants. I am a freshman who believes a Congressman ought to know what goes on in a public agency; I am such a freshman that I do not believe the head of a civilian agency should act like a military commander and order 250 civilian families to pick up and move their homes without showing good cause. In short, I am one to stay a "freshman" all his life, if Mr. Halaby is an example of how sophomores are supposed to act.[13]

---

[12]U.S., Congressional Record, 88th Cong., 2d Sess., 1962, pp. 13999-55508, A5855-5955.

[13]Henry B. Gonzalez, "The Congressman From Bexar Reports," June, 1962.

In addition to his vigorous public protests, Gonzalez appeared
before the appropriations subcommittee which has jurisdiction over the
FAA budget; he protested Halaby's decision to the President; he asked
the Comptroller General to investigate the accuracy of FAA figures submitted to justify the move; he requested the Bureau of the Budget to
explain its knowledge of the proposed change; he asked the General
Services Administration, which has jurisdiction over the maintenance
of federal property, to investigate plans for abandonment of the New
Orleans FAA building; and he met with various congressional leaders to
enlist their support. In San Antonio, he received a cross-section of
community support in his fight against Halaby.

National coverage was extended to his challenge as newspapers
throughout the country reported his drive to oust Halaby. Individuals
from across the nation who, for various reasons, had been experiencing
difficulties with the FAA began to write Gonzalez and report inconsistencies to him. Various congressmen began to question Halaby when
Gonzalez revealed that the administrator was withholding information
as to the location of 100 proposed safety installations for which he
had requested appropriations. Gonzalez reasoned "that it was entirely
proper that a congressman who is being asked to vote on an appropriation bill should want to know where certain projects are to be
built. . . ."[14]

---

[14]Henry B. Gonzalez, news release, August 8, 1962.

Halaby's refusal to reveal information to Gonzalez involved an issue that has caused friction between the executive and legislative branches from time to time. One can recall several instances when the executive has maintained that certain information was "privileged" and would not be given to members of the Congress.

However, executive privilege is traditionally invoked by members of the cabinet or by the President himself, but seldom by the administrator of an independent agency. Furthermore, the privilege is customarily associated with the executive's opinion that revelation of information would be detrimental to the national interest as he interprets it. According to Gonzalez, in Halaby's case, the question was not protection of the national interest but protection of Halaby's interests.

Gonzalez was successful in delaying the proposed move from June, 1964, to June, 1965. Then, on April 26, 1965, President Johnson announced at his press conference that retired Air Force General William F. McKee would become the new Administrator of the Federal Aviation Agency. The announcement was sudden, and no mention was made of Halaby's resignation or of his future plans. The circumstances surrounding the announcement led reporters to conclude that Halaby had been fired, since it is customary to give some information concerning the resigning official's future--that is, if he is actually resigning.

There is little doubt that Halaby's removal was due greatly to Gonzalez' efforts against him. Gonzalez had vowed to settle the issue with "decent regard for the needs of national air safety, governmental economy, the rights of civilian employees, the interests of San Antonio, and the proper role of a government bureaucrat in a democracy."[15] He had read into the Record accounts of air collisions and crashes that, he said, were partially due to Halaby's inability to administer his agency properly. Gonzalez also reasoned that, even if the proposed move had been feasible before, the circumstances had changed with Johnson's elevation to the presidency. Because of the increased air traffic to nearby Austin occasioned by the President's visits home, there was, according to Gonzalez, a vital need to maintain the air safety of the area, which was serviced by the San Antonio center.

The night before his announcement, the President called Gonzalez to tell him of the decision to remove Halaby. Johnson indicated that one of the major reasons for this action was Gonzalez' efforts in making public the inconsistencies in Halaby's administration. Reporter Sarah McClendon, in a story credited "to the highest authority," indicated that Gonzalez had been partially responsible for Halaby's removal.[16] This writer has since learned that Miss McClendon spoke to the President about the removal but did not reveal her source publicly.

Throughout his criticisms of Halaby, Gonzalez emphasized the need of establishing definite safeguards to prevent an agency from acting summarily and without public accountability. He did not limit

---

[15]Ibid.

[16]San Antonio Light, April 30, 1965.

his discussion to the FAA, since he felt that all public agencies had to be responsible to the public. He had argued for this while on the city council in asking that a city utilities department be established and in the Senate he had introduced legislation requiring all public agencies to hold public meeting. He reasoned that governmental agencies had, by their very nature, an impact on the economy of the community in which they operated. Sudden and arbitrary action to move or close the agency could have serious effects on the local economy. Thus, Gonzalez introduced H.R. 2334 which required federal civilian agency heads to notify congressmen concerning the closing or moving of installations and providing for public hearings in that regard.

In a related field, he introduced a resolution to establish a joint committee on foreign information and intelligence to make continuing studies of the activities and problems of agencies such as the Civilian Intelligence Agency. Again, Gonzalez' belief that governmental agencies should be subject to certain controls is visible. He does not believe that an agency should be allowed the power to act without providing Congress and the public with information on the reasons and factors surrounding its actions. This shows his a basic trust in democracy. It also shows Gonzalez' belief in the dignity of the individual.

Gonzalez' respect for the individual prompted him to react sharply when two civil service employees at Kelly Air Force Base were suspended for giving him information on work loads. The men were suspended summarily without hearings. Gonzalez challenged the Secretary of the Air Force to uphold the action under the Constitution and demanded that the men be reinstated with back pay and that their records be cleared. He said the men were being punished for exercising their constitutional right of writing to their congressman. The Secretary agreed, rescinded the order, and restored the men their jobs with back pay and clear records. Gonzalez maintains that every citizen has the right to write his congressman and not be arbitrarily punished for it.

San Antonians are well aware of Gonzalez' belief that they should write to him and they do so constantly. In 1962 he received 50,000 letters, including congratulatory ones on his election. The average mail received is about 125 letters per day including Saturdays and Sundays. Filling the requests that are usually included in the letters constitutes work required in the congressional role referred to as "errand-boy." The requests vary from pleas for assistance in obtaining a veteran's pension to research material for a graduate student.

In his final newsletter of the 87th Congress, Gonzalez indicated his views on his role as an errand-boy:

> I see a congressman's duty as more than that of representative of the people for legislative purposes. In our present structure of government, he is also an expediter, a man to help you cut through red tape and bureaucratic mish-mash, to get action and answers from governmental agencies.[17]

---

[17]Henry B. Gonzalez, "The Congressman From Bexar Reports," October, 1962.

To help him expedite and cut through red tape, Gonzalez has a staff of eight in Washington. It is a young staff as no member has reached the age of thirty. The staff is alert and aggressive, making up in ingenuity what it lacks in experience. It is devoted and loyal to Gonzalez and the district. Case mail is handled by various staff members and is controlled by Gonzalez with his signature. Each letter that he signs--and he signs them all personally--has attached to it the case file for his review.

Case load in Gonzalez' office is well above the average. An illustration is the volume of Air Force cases, which, in 1962, averaged twenty-five per month. According to the Air Force Legislative Liaison office an average of about twelve cases per month were received from each House member. This indicates that Gonzalez' Air Force case load is twice the congressional average. His staff is certain that the same result applies to his case mail on other matters. Success in helping constituents varies, but Gonzalez feels he is successful in about one-third of the cases. However, he agrees with congressional concensus that "it is not the percentages which are important but the fact that occasionally an injustice is corrected."[18]

Gonzalez' local office in San Antonio also aids him in his role as errand-boy. Many of the visits and calls that the San Antonio office receives are from constituents who do not speak English, or who

---

[18]Charles L. Clapp, The Congressman (Garden City, New York: Anchor Books, Doubleday & Company, Inc., 1964), p. 87.

are functional illiterates. These people find it difficult, if not impossible, to write. Thus, by contacting the district office, they can enlist Gonzalez' aid without writing to him. The office receives an average of thirty telephone calls per day and is visited by at least twelve constituents each day. The district office also serves as news gathering center for Gonzalez as it is in communication with him or his Washington staff daily.

In addition to the case mail and requests for information about legislation, Gonzalez receives letters from businessmen in San Antonio who have dealings with the government. To help these and other businessmen Gonzalez established a special position on his staff. All inquiries and requests for assistance in business matters are channeled through the "Business Development" section of his office, which, in reality, is his research assistant. The emphasis placed on business development by Gonzalez reflects his determination to help shift a portion of the economic foundation of the district from the governmental to the private sector. At a meeting with businessmen in San Antonio, he said: "I've got to be realistic enough to realize that some federal complexes in San Antonio will eventually be phased out."[19]

When he assumed office he saw the awesome responsibility of protecting the interests of the district in Washington. The vast military complexes provided Bexar County with 40 per cent of its economy. He realized that advanced technology and automation could easily

---

[19]Morris Willson, "Bexar Facts" San Antonio Light, May 3, 1965.

deprive San Antonio of its number one employer--Kelly Air Force Base.
He also saw that he was in a position to help unite the community,
which was divided economically and culturally. Thus he called on San
Antonio to "take its very diversity and make it a source of strength."[20]

He dramatized the issue by calling for a "Twentieth Century
Program for the Twentieth District." He seized upon the idea of conducting a "Fair of the Americas" in commemoration of the 250th anniver-
sary of the founding of San Antonio. The idea was not new, but Gonzalez grasped the concept, convinced a group of local businessmen that
it would succeed, and now the entire state is conscious of the potential of the Hemisfair. Gonzalez believed that San Antonio with its
cultural diversity and proximity to Latin America, could attract
exhibits and patrons from the countries of the Western Hemisphere.
The exhibits and permanent buildings would then give San Antonio a new
source of economic revenue. Hemisfair is scheduled to begin in 1968
and is well ahead of its projected schedule for completion. Land for
the Fair is now being purchased with urban renewal funds Gonzalez
helped obtain.

After he initiated interest in the Hemisfair, Gonzalez, with
the aid of the San Antonio River Authority, revived the idea of investigating the feasibility of constructing a barge canal from San
Antonio to the intercoastal canal in the Gulf of Mexico. He succeeded
in obtaining the necessary appropriations for the study and the results

---

[20]San Antonio News, June 19, 1962.

will be made public shortly after this paper is written. If a canal is built, heavy industry could be attracted to San Antonio, thus relieving some of its economic dependency on the military complexes.

Gonzalez has also succeeded in obtaining $68,000,000 in construction projects for San Antonio including a new federal office building and post office, a veterans' hospital, and funds for a medical and teaching hospital. Although these projects are not yet completed, all are at least in the planning stage or have been approved by the administration. Impact of these projects on the San Antonio economy, is estimated to be about $204,000,000.[21] This again, illustrates his efforts to shift the economic base away from the military complexes.

There have been a series of other projects that, while not as spectacular, have contributed to San Antonio's economy. These include a favorable decision from the Internal Revenue Service which exempts Mexican nationals from paying excise taxes on goods purchased in San Antonio stores; an increase in pay to wage board employees of civil service which added $5,300,000 into San Antonio's economy. This resulted from a special request by Gonzalez for a survey to determine why San Antonio wage board employees were receiving a lower rate of pay than those in Corpus Christi.

Interrelated with his duties as an errand-boy and protector of San Antonio economy is Gonzalez' role as creator of public opinion.

---

[21]Staff memorandum to Henry B. Gonzalez, April 7, 1965.

In order to proceed with his "Twentieth Century Program for the Twentieth District," Gonzalez was forced to create the proper atmosphere for his projects. To him the problem was not what to do, but how to do it? In his early career he had created public opinion raising a well-informed voice and taking the issues to the people. He had been a constructive irritant. In Congress his programs and policies would depend on how he performed. He no longer was an underdog fighting an uphill battle; he was now an established and influential public official. He chose to soften·his sometimes critical tones and not to antagonize unduly.

Gonzalez is possessed with talents that allow him to communicate easily with people. He can express himself freely and paint clear pictures in explanation of complex issues and policies. His adeptness at reporting on television and acknowledged oratorical ability allow him to convince listeners of the merits of his case. Yet, his most effective tool is information. He makes special efforts and financial sacrifice in order to keep San Antonians informed as fully as possible.

Weekly radio and television reports are Gonzalez' most consistent techniques of informing constituents. He broadcasts over both radio and television in Spanish and English, and has spent a large amount of his salary to pay for the film and the use of the studio in Washington. His television reports are for fifteen minutes. He explains important events of the week and sometimes discusses major issues with guests. He has had as guests several members of the cabinet, agency heads, ambassadors, foreign dignitaries, and other national legislators. His guests always assure the audience that they have a particular interest in San Antonio because of Gonzalez' tenaciousness. Viewers are often informed of facts they would never know otherwise. On radio he presents a five-minute show usually dealing with one issue of importance each week.

Gonzalez publishes a newsletter periodically and sends it to 50,000 people. His mailing list is one of the largest in the House. The newsletter is considered one of the most attractive and readable because of the layout. Most congressional newsletters are letter-like and treat a limited number of topics. Gonzalez' newsletters are four to six pages long with varied type, and include photographs. In certain instances he has mailed out 100,000 copies of one issue at a cost of $900 for paper alone.

The newsletter maintains a running account of Gonzalez' votes on major legislation, status of bills he has introduced, progress reports on government projects in San Antonio, and general information of interest to constituents. In addition, he has attempted to educate as well as to inform constituents by providing special series on specific aspects of government. One was a five part series on federal financing including charts and graphs; a second, was a two part series on the legislative process explaining the committee system and the steps bills must go through before becoming law.

A key factor in his effectiveness as a creator of public opinion is the fact that he returns to the district almost every weekend.

In 1962 he returned to San Antonio fifty-six times, in 1963 he returned
to San Antonio sixty-three times, and in 1964 he traveled home on forty-
three occasions. When he returns to the district, it is usually on a
commercial flight, although occasionally he is able to fly with the
President to Austin. Plane fare must come from Gonzalez' own pocket
unless an organization or group he addresses pays for his transportation. While in San Antonio he attends public functions, makes speeches,
and meets with political, civic, and business leaders. Individuals
and groups who talk with him have an opportunity to obtain information
that only Gonzalez, as a congressman, can give them. This factor in
itself does much to create a favorable opinion for issues and projects
Gonzalez is interested in supporting.

A routine, yet important, technique of creating public opinion
is Gonzalez' use of press releases. Timing is the key to an effective
news release and Gonzalez is adept at this aspect of the technique.
For example, prior to the 1964 election, Gonzalez showered the local
press with releases on special projects and grants-in-aid for San
Antonio. Although he had developed a keen sense of news-making as a
city councilman, Vice-President Johnson further impressed Gonzalez
with the importance of maintaining a steady stream of news releases.
In a visit to the LBJ Ranch, Gonzalez and three of his staff members
had a conversation with Johnson about the necessity of creating a good
public image in the first 100 days in office. Johnson advised them it
was necessary to keep the public informed of their congressman's

achievements so that they would be of the opinion that their representative in Washington was doing a good job.[22]

On several occasions, either by fate or by design, Gonzalez has attracted national news coverage and carried his role as a creator of public opinion across the United States. In a sense he has become a national congressman, or as is indicated to Henry Wilson, a White House aide, on the inscription of a calendar Gonzalez gave him, "from Henry Gonzalez, your national congressman at large."[23] The New York Times recognized Gonzalez' national interest when they endorsed his reelection because he was one of ten congressmen who had consistently voted in the national interest over local or sectional interests.[24] Besides voting for the national interest, Gonzalez has also acted in the national interest and created favorable opinion.

He has conducted a nationwide campaign against the arming of right-wing groups by the Department of Defense. Shortly after his vote against appropriations for the House Committee on Un-American Activities, the national publication of a group called the Minutemen, On Target, published the names of the twenty congressmen who voted with Gonzalez in black bordered box labeled "In Memoriam." After President Kennedy's assassination, Gonzalez became alarmed at the warning. He

---

[22]Interview with Gail Beagle, Executive Secretary for Henry B. Gonzalez, April 7, 1965.

[23]Calendar seen in office of Henry Wilson by the writer.

[24]November 1, 1964.

wrote Chief Justice Earl Warren and asked that the commission investigating the President's death not overlook groups like the Minutemen. Gonzalez also asked Attorney General Robert Kennedy to investigate the activities of the Minutemen to see if they had violated any federal statutes. Gonzalez released the texts of these letters to the press and they were given national attention.

Later, Gonzalez asked the Department of Defense for information concerning the distribution of weapons and ammunition to civilian organizations because the Minutemen had boasted of their members being supplied with surplus materials. The Department revealed that the Army was spending $12,000,000 annually to supply civilian groups and individuals through the National Rifle Association. Gonzalez then made numerous press releases and insertions in the Record attaching right-wing groups like the Minutemen and criticizing the Army's policy of loosely providing them with supplies. The New Republic, The Progressive, Harpers, The New York Times, The Washington Post, and many local newspapers throughout the country commented editorially in support of Gonzalez' position. Finally, the Executive Vice-President of the National Rifle Association said that the organization would start double-checking its membership in an effort to eliminate any members of extremist groups. He admitted that the association "has been taking a beating" because of alleged links between it and such groups.[25]

---

[25] San Antonio News, April 30, 1965.

In another project, Gonzalez acted both as legislator and as
public opinion maker. This was on the question of the use of foreign
labor to harvest agricultural crops through Public Law 78. Gonzalez
maintained that braceros brought into this country were working under
conditions similar to slave labor, and, in addition, were preventing
the native agricultural migrant workers from competing freely for jobs.
The program had been in effect since 1941 and had been periodically
renewed without serious difficulty. However, the law was coming under
increasing criticism from some congressmen and senators. Gonzalez led
the fight in the House to prevent extension of the law and almost succeeded. One of the crucial moments was in a speech Gonzalez delivered
in the House against the extension. The speech was a highly emotional
and informative one, and it quieted the usually noisy chamber. After
the speech, a Republican came up to Gonzalez and told him that he had
always voted for the bill, not knowing exactly what it meant, but
after listening to him, he would vote against the extension.[26] The
House first voted not to extend the bracero program but pressure from
lobbyists forced them to reconsider and a one-year extension was
approved. During the debate on the question, which lasted for several weeks, Gonzalez made numerous, almost daily, insertions in the
Record pointing to the evils of the bracero program. He also made
almost daily press releases in which he recounted the plight of migrant
workers as a result of the bracero program.

---

[26]Interview with Henry B. Gonzalez, December 18, 1964.

In two separate incidents, Gonzalez attracted publicity by
reacting sharply to individuals questioning his integrity. The first
was in relation to a newspaper interview by former Republican Representative Ed Foreman of Odessa, Texas, in which he questioned Gonzalez'
patriotism and referred to him as a "pinko." Gonzalez questioned Foreman
about the statement during a session of the House. When Foreman reacted
sarcastically, Gonzalez asked him to step outside and there gave him a
verbal lashing and shoved him for emphasis. Foreman darted back into
the chamber and Gonzalez went to lunch. Foreman then wen to the news
media and complained that Gonzalez had attacked him forcibly. The
incident became the lead story in most newscasts and newspapers throughout the country. Gonzalez denied having hit Foreman but did admit
that he had been irritated by Foreman's statements. Gonzalez reasoned
that Foreman was resorting to the smears tactics of irresponsible
people. He said that, as a politician he could take verbal abuse, but
not from a colleague. Gonzalez added that Foreman's tactics were
uncalled for in the Congress. Many newspapers throughout the country
editorially supported Gonzalez' position. Foreman ceased his verbal
questioning of the patriotism of Gonzalez and other congressmen.
After attempting to explain his position on the House floor, Foreman's
remarks were ordered struck from the record.

The second incident occurred several months before it was made
public by Representative Patman in a speech critical of the national
banking lobby. Patman revealed that a member of his committee had
been offered $14,000 in bank stock and had turned it down. Upon

questioning, Gonzalez admitted that it was he. He explained that a
San Antonio banker had offered a position on the board of directors of
a local national bank along with the stock because of its publicity
value to his bank. Gonzalez did not allow the individual to explain
further as he invited him to leave the office. Patman heard of the
incident when Gonzalez' legislative assistant related the story to a
staff member of the Banking and Currency Committee.

Gonzalez said that he though that acceptance of the offer
would constitute a conflict of interests since he was a member of the
committee which regulated the operations of banks. The matter attracted
editorial comment throughout the country, as editors applauded Gonzalez'
integrity. Gonzalez received letters of commendation from all parts
of the United States, from Latin America, and Europe. He said that it
was not a difficult decision for him to make because whenever such an
offer is made, the answer must be no, if it is apparent that it was
motivated by his public position.

In 1962 he was unopposed in the Democratic Primary and in the
General Election. Gonzalez did not have much difficulty in gaining
reelection in 1964. His opponent was John O'Connell, a lawyer who had
been in San Antonio for ten years. The campaign was not as tense and
emotional as some of Gonzalez' previous campaigns, primarily because
O'Connell, a Republican, was given little chance of winning. Gonzalez,
never one to accept things for granted, campaigned throughout the district and used many of the campaign techniques he has learned and
mastered through years of electioneering.

Actually, Gonzalez is a perpetual campaigner, always shaking hands, making witty remarks, remembering names and events, making appearances, performing duties of the errand-boy type, conducting special mailings, unveiling special projects for San Antonio, and performing the various other roles of a campaigner. In other words, Gonzalez is consistently in the public eye, usually in a favorable light.

Nonetheless, Gonzalez did intensify his campaigning as the election neared. He appeared on a series of television programs, saturated the city with bumper stickers and campaign posters, and visited union halls, factory shift changes, community shopping centers, and business establishments. He ignored his opponent and concentrated on his record of "achievement and hard work." In newspaper advertisements and in public speeches he emphasized his record of accomplishments while in office. In speeches to Latin-American audiences he reminded them that it was their hard work and support that allowed "the Henry Gonzalezes to go to Washington" to represent them.

Since 1964 was a presidential election year, Gonzalez was again asked to campaign for the national Democratic ticket. He served as National Co-chairman of the Viva Johnson Clubs with U.S. Representatives Ed Roybal of California and Joe Montoya of New Mexico. He traveled in eleven states campaigning for the Johnson-Humphery ticket and made campaign talks in ten cities in Texas. In San Antonio he was unofficial coordinator of the Democratic campaign. Local state legislative candidates were experiencing a heavily financed campaign against them and Gonzalez made special efforts to help them. He planned and participated in a series of television programs on the Democratic ticket in Bexar County. On election eve, he conducted an eight-hour telethon from 11:00 P.M. to 7:00 A.M. election morning. He devoted most of the time to answering questions from viewers who called in. He explained the key issues of the Democratic platform, defended the budgetary policy of the administration, explained his vote on the House Committee on Un-American Activities, and answered in detail each question asked. In the telethon he exhibited a knowledge and understanding of a vast number of political issues and governmental programs.

Gonzalez won the election by receiving 100,000 votes to O'Connell's 55,000. It was the highest number of votes Gonzalez has received in an election in San Antonio. In all sections of the city Gonzalez surpassed all previous totals. He carried 136 of the county's 171 precincts; 36 of them he carried by margins of more than 90 per cent of the votes cast; in 74 precincts his margin was 70 per cent or more of the votes; he lost only 16 precincts with 30 per cent or fewer votes. The most revealing figures in the election are the result of eighteen North Side precincts usually considered Republican strongholds. In these precincts Gonzalez received only 31 per cent of the vote against John Goode in 1961; in 1964 he received 45 per cent of the votes.

Results of the 1964 election indicate that Gonzalez convinced the vast majority of San Antonio voters, no matter what their ethnic, social, or economic background, that he is an effective congressman and deserves their support. He has accomplished this by hard work and

by producing results for the district. From time to time criticisms
are made of his votes, his actions, or his statements; at other times
criticisms are made of his lack of action or failure to make statements; however, Gonzalez has thus far been able to convince most people
that he is doing a good job as congressman.

CHAPTER VI

FORMULA FOR SUCCESS

The political career of Henry B. Gonzalez has been tradition-breaking as well as eventful and colorful. Because certain barriers and traditions have now been removed, it is possible for others to follow in Gonzalez' steps. With some guidelines to follow, interested individuals could even surpass Gonzalez' achievements. A comprehensive answer to reasons for his success cannot be provided, as there are variables involved that cannot be fully explained or understood. It is possible, however, to point out certain techniques, principles, and circumstances that contributed to his political achievements. Since it would be difficult to set down an ideal set of circumstances that an aspiring politician could conform to, mention will be made of techniques and principles used by Gonzalez so that the reader can adapt those that are most suitable.

There is little doubt that Gonzalez' bicultural background has been an asset rather than a hindrance. If Gonzalez had not experienced the humiliations of discrimination, or had not endured the tragedies of poverty at The University of Texas, it is likely that he would not have been driven to reach the success that he has. Certainly this is not to say that he would not have succeeded as an Anglo, but, rather, that a minority status gave him more to strive for. However, because he was completely versed in the traditions of two cultures, Gonzalez was able to span the gulf between them and build a bridge of understanding. In campaigns he has been able to establish a rapport with audiences because he can draw from either of his cultures to suit the occasion.

There are a great many maxims that could be set down to illustrate and dramatize guidelines on Gonzalez' success; however, it is best to discuss the man and not rules. Perhaps the most penetrating statement about Gonzalez' principles is that people are more important to him than traditions. Thus, if a tradition allows an injustice to occur, he will ignore tradition to correct the injustice. Along with this disbelief in the sacredness of traditions, Gonzalez combines a belief in the virtue of being straightforward in dealings with people. Gonzalez told this writer that he learned several things from the late Judge Charles Anderson. Positively, he learned to always go out to meet people; negatively, he learned never to vacillate with people. Anyone who has had conversations with Gonzalez is aware that he is always straightforward when the occasion demands it.

A key to Gonzalez' success has been his ability to convert ideas into action. Although he is not a philosopher, he has an understanding of the subject. More important, he can act on principles of philosophy. He can take the concept of the rights of man and apply it to a beggar on the streets, or take the idea of the responsibilities of the bureaucrat in a democracy and apply it to a Najeeb Halaby.

Although the process appears simple at first glance, it requires a facility of mind to apply it properly.

His success on the city council and in the State Senate illustrates that an underdog who studies and learns, not only the details of his project, but the nature of his battle and the ways to win it, will confound and distract his opponent to the point of despair. In challenging the power structure, however, one must be fully equipped with the facts, since a défeat at that point can be more damaging than not having challenged at all. The power structure will be able to eliminate its vulnerable positions if it is warned of their existence.

Timing is an important factor in Gonzalez' success. This is an asset that one must cultivate and develop. Gonzalez' career has been marked by a series of steps taken at the proper time. For example, his move into the State Senate was timed perfectly. It is entirely possible that if Gonzalez had waited another election before attempting a move up in politics, that he would not be a congressman today. Along with a sense of timing, an individual should have the patience to withhold information or facts at times in order to use them more effectively at a later time. In Gonzalez' words, "Don't shoot all your guns at once; you never know when you'll need them again."

Probably one of Gonzalez' most perfected techniques is that of pinpointing and selecting the areas of discussion and controversy. His first rule is to avoid making wholesale condemnations. He reasons that the more widespread your allegations, the more difficult they are to defend. People are interested in specifics and they will respond to them more quickly than to generalizations.

In order to be effective, an individual cannot be involved in factional disputes. Incidental or petty disputes must be avoided. This is especially true when the dispute involves groups or individuals who are both friendly to you. In an effort to aid one of the disputants, the individual can lose the loyalty of the other. This appears to be fence-straddling, but it is not, if one remembers that the key here is that one of the disputants is not an arch enemy. By taking a position apart from factionalism, the individual can influence both sides to see things his way.

Of course, there are some rules that are obvious, such as the necessity of hard work, of taking nothing for granted, and a love and understanding of people. One must also develop an oratorical ability, a penetrating wit, and a tenacity of purpose. It helps also to be a prolific reader so that one might learn from books what he cannot learn from people.

Once an office of public trust is assumed, an individual must take on the responsibilities as well as the glories. The true test of a man in public life is how he acts while in an office of responsibility. He must be a representative of all the people, not just of those who voted for him or of those who he feels an affinity to. At times one must act as a referee rather than as a protagonist or antagonist. And to many this is the most difficult role to play. A public official has a duty to develop an ability to listen to the views of everyone and

157

only then to make a decision on legislation or in the execution of a program. This does not mean that one must compromise his principles; it only means that in order to exercise one's judgment properly and effectively, it is best to first be aware of all the facts and opinions surrounding the issue.

The final test of a good public official is what he leaves behind. Are things and conditions better than when the official assumed responsibility for them? Are more people interested in justice and equality than before he assumed office? Has the individual official sacrificed his principles? If good can be accomplished, has it been accomplished? The best monument for a public figure is the one in peoples' hearts, and it will last as long as the people want it to.

The people have shown that Henry B. Gonzalez is in their hearts because they know they are constantly on his mind.

BIBLIOGRAPHY

BIBLIOGRAPHY

Public Documents

U.S. Bureau of the Census. <u>Fifteenth Census of the United States:</u>
<u>1930. Population</u>, Vol. II.

_____. <u>Sixteenth Census of the United States: 1940. Population</u>,
Vol. II.

_____. <u>Seventeenth Census of the United States: 1950. Popula-</u>
<u>tion</u>, Vol. II.

U.S. <u>Congressional Record</u>. Vols. CVII, CVIII, CIX, CX.

Books

Burns, James MacGregor. <u>Roosevelt: The Lion and the Fox</u>. New York:
Harcourt, Brace & World, Inc., 1956.

Castañeda, Carlos E. <u>Our Catholic Heritage in Texas, 1519-1936</u>.
Vol. I: <u>The Mission Era: The Finding of Texas, 1519-1693</u>.
Austin: Von Boeckmann-Jones Co., 1936.

Clapp, Charles L. <u>The Congressman</u>. Garden City, New York: Anchor
Books, Doubleday & Company, Inc., 1964.

Federal Writers' Project Works Progress Administration. ("American
Guide Series") <u>San Antonio, An Authoritative Guide to the</u>
<u>City and Its Environs</u>. San Antonio: The Clegg Co., 1938.

Gantt, Fred, Jr. <u>The Chief Executive in Texas</u>. Austin: The University of Texas Press, 1964.

House, Boyce. <u>City of Flaming Adventure</u>. San Antonio: The Naylor
Company, 1949.

Peyton, Green. <u>San Antonio, City in the Sun</u>. New York: Wittlesey
House, 1946.

Ramsdell, Charles. <u>San Antonio</u>. Austin: The University of Texas
Press, 1959.

Articles and Periodicals

Close, Kathryn. "Sick Men Can't Fight," Survey Graphic, reprint (March, 1943), 1-6.

Congressional Quarterly Almanac, 88th Congress, 1st Session. Vol. XIX. Washington, D.C.: Congressional Quarterly Service, 1963.

Congressional Quarterly, October 30, 1964.

Dugger, Ronnie. "Filibusters and Majority Rule," The Progressive, (August, 1947), p. 21.

Handman, Max. "San Antonio, The Old Capital City of Mexican Life and Influence," The Survey, LXVI (May 1, 1931), 163-166.

Stilwell, Hart. "Texas Rebel With a Cause," Coronet, (August, 1958), pp. 43-47.

"Texas: For Whom the Bell Tolls," Time, (May 13, 1957), p. 27.

White, Owen P. "Machine Made," Colliers, (September 18, 1937), p. unk.

Reports

American Public Welfare Association. Public Welfare Survey of San Antonio, Texas. Chicago: American Public Welfare Association, 1940.

Community Welfare Council. Recreation: An Essential Community Service. San Antonio, 1954. (Mimeographed.)

Department of Health, City of San Antonio. City Health Department, 1946-1947. 1947.

Housing Authority, City of San Antonio. San Antonio Housing Survey. 1939.

Planning Department, City of San Antonio. Economic Base Study of San Antonio, Texas. 1964.

San Antonio Public Service Company. An Economic and Industrial Survey of San Antonio, Texas. 1942. (Mimeographed.)

Newspapers

Militant American. 1964.

New York Times. 1964.

San Antonio Express. 1953-1965.

San Antonio Light. 1931-1965.

San Antonio News. 1934-1965.

San Antonio Register. 1949.

The Texas Observer. 1956-1965.

The Washington Post. 1934-1965.

Interviews

Gonzalez, Henry B., U.S. Representative. 1964-1965.

Gonzalez, Dr. Joaquin, brother of Henry B. Gonzalez. February, 1965.

Gonzalez, Leonides, father of Henry B. Gonzalez. June, 1964.

Gonzalez, Mrs. Henry B. February, 1965.

Retired schoolteacher and Gonzalez supporter. April, 1965.

Schnabel, Charles, Secretary of Senate of Texas, Austin, Texas. November, 1964.

Supporter of Henry B. Gonzalez. February, 1965.

Other Sources

Gonzalez, Henry B. Files, Correspondence, and Scrapbooks.

Cases

Clifton v. Puente (CA) 218 SW 2d 272 (1948) Texas Court of Appeals.

Hernandez v. Texas 347 U.S. 475 (1954).

EPILOGUE

Since 1965 many events have occurred which have changed the mood
and temper of the country. The Great Society of Lyndon Johnson has
been followed by the New Federalism of Richard Nixon and the caretaker
programs of Gerald Ford. Aggressive government efforts to improve standards of living have been replaced by national policies designed to
"Whip Inflation Now (WIN)" by reducing the level of federal government
involvement in solving local problems.

Armed conflict and then peace in Vietnam have been accompanied by
traumatic divisions between young and older generations. Economic growth
and stability have been replaced by stagflation, a paradox of inflation
in the midst of recession. A world of plenty has been shrouded by a veil
of scarcity in natural resources. The crescendos of the civil rights
movement have been lowered to subtle, but persisting tones now heard among
numerous minority groups and women.

Political assassinations have numbed consciences. Corrupt and
illegal use of government power and influence has resulted in the shame-
ful resignations of a President and Vice President. National opinion
polls reflect a loss of confidence and trust in government institutions
which apparently result from public expectations that government should
alleviate, not exacerbate problems. Under these conditions, individuals
in elective offices must meet high public standards to avoid defeat or
worse yet, public apathy and loss of confidence.

Henry B. Gonzalez has continued to represent the Twentieth District
of Texas, the heart of San Antonio, during this tumultuous ten-year period.

His record as a national legislator, a Democratic party leader, a public
educator, and a protector of local public interests can be reviewed
and examined in the light of current public standards. Therefore, a
brief commentary of the Gonzalez record during the last ten years is
necessary to provide a contemporary perspective. The following comments,
while not all inclusive, should serve as a general guide to the inter-
vening period since the original work was written.

As a national legislator, Gonzalez has been developing experience
and stature during his fourteen years in Washington. Within the House
Democratic structure, he has risen to the position of Zone Whip for
Texas. In this capacity, he serves as one of twenty Democratic members
of the House who work with the majority leadership and members of their
Zones on upcoming votes in the House. He is still a member of the
Banking, Currency and Housing Committee and its Housing, Consumer Affairs
and General Oversight and Renegotiation Subcommittees. Gonzalez is
building seniority in the Congress and as a result is now Chairman of
the Banking Committee's Subcommittee on International Monetary Institutions and Finance. He is Chairman of the Ad Hoc Subcommittee on the
Robinson-Patman Act, Antitrust and Related Matters of the new Committee
on Small Business and the ranking member of the Select Committee of the
Missing in Southeast Asia.

Students of Congress maintain that the most important legislative
work is conducted in subcommittee and committee activities. If this pre-
mise is accepted, then Gonzalez' legislative work is centered on issues
and problems that relate directly to the heart of his constituency, the

poor, the middle-income earners, and small business people. All of these groups are affected by the nation's fiscal and monetary policies which are under constant review by the Banking, Currency and Housing Committee. His position on the Housing and Consumer Affairs Subcommittees reflects his interest in these issues as does his role as Chairman of the Subcommittee on the Robinson-Patman Act (a law designed to protect small businesses from unfair buying and selling practices).

In recent years, Gonzalez has developed a special interest in international monetary institutions such as the World Bank, The African Development Fund, the Inter-American Development Bank and the Asian Development Bank. The U. S. policies and practices on financial loans and assistance to developing countries are a major concern to Gonzalez who believes that the nation has a responsibility to help these countries in their development efforts. As Chairman of the House Subcommittee responsible for overseeing the U. S. role in international monetary institutions, he has assumed a major responsibility that reaches far beyond the limits of his congressional district.

As a member of the motorcade that accompanied John F. Kennedy the day he was assassinated in Dallas, Gonzalez directly and personally experienced the tragedy. The subsequent assassinations of Senator Robert Kennedy and the Reverend Martin Luther King and the attempts on Governor George Wallace and President Ford have prompted Gonzalez to sponsor legislation to establish a select committee of the House to study recent political assassinations in the United States. Gonzalez believes that until the assassinations are thoroughly reviewed in terms of their institutional and societal causes, as well as their specific

causes, it will be difficult to prevent them in the future. He believes
that unless further, more definitive study is conducted, the continuing
uncertainty and persisting conspiratorial theories surrounding the assassinations could undermine the basic fabric of democratic government.

This interest in protecting the basic foundation of democratic
government has been a consistent aspect of Gonzalez' approach to his
legislative duties. It prompted him in the Texas Senate to oppose the
segregation bills which were later ruled unconstitutional. It has led
him to oppose the Twenty Fifth Amendment which provides for the presidential appointment of a Vice President. He believes that by permitting
a small group of individuals to turn over the Presidency to a person not
elected by the people, future elections can be manipulated to thwart
the democratic process. Consistent with his opposition to the Amendment,
Gonzalez voted against Gerald Ford's confirmation as Vice President and
the subsequent appointment of Nelson Rockefellar as his successor. Now
an unelected President has the vast power of incumbency in the 1976
Presidential elections. Gonzalez does not believe this to be a healthy
situation in a democracy regardless of the honesty and integrity of the
unelected incumbent.

The Vietnam conflict also presented Gonzalez with a constitutional
dilemma. While he agreed that U. S. troops needed basic support, he
also believed that the constitutional crisis concerning the powers of
Congress to declare war and the powers of the President as Commander-in-
Chief needed resolution. His answer was to sponsor a bill to deny the
Executive authority to send draftees into combat areas except in declared
wars. Thus, while many viewed the domestic conflict over Vietnam as a

social and political problem, Gonzalez perceived a basic constitutional question which he proposed to resolve by denying the President authority over draftees.

These and other national and global changes have been accompanied by simultaneous adjustments in the social and political climate of San Antonio. When considering local changes, it is particularly important to determine how much Gonzalez has influenced the city's social and political environment in the last ten years. In other words, what influence has Gonzalez had in San Antonio since 1965?

There is little doubt that Gonzalez has become the dominant political figure in San Antonio. This phenomenon is unusual in the traditional sense of political power since he has achieved this position without the benefit of extensive patronage or political organization. He is still essentially a "one man band" who deals with people and issues on a one to one basis. Perhaps his most potent weapon is an ability to command public attention on issues he considers important. He has an innate ability to identify issues, focus attention, and inform the public about them that is unmatched by any local official. This helps him rally public opinion in support of his positions. Individuals or groups who challenge Gonzalez on public issues often find themselves defending their own positions from an onslaught of public opinion. Thus, without an extensive organization, Gonzalez still commands attention more than any other individual or group in the public arena. No doubt the basic skills he developed during his formative years by doing his homework, carefully picking the issues, perfecting the timing and supporting the public over special interest have served him well in the local political arena.

Since 1965, Henry B. Gonzalez has been re-elected to Congress
seven times. At the time of this writing (March, 1976), he is unopposed
in the Democratic primary and there is no Republican candidate to
oppose him in the General Election. In fact, since the 1964 campaign,
Gonzalez has not been seriously challenged in his bids for re-election.
Most serious political observers acknowledge that under current circumstances an election challenge to Gonzalez would be tantamount to political suicide. The question is, why?

There are two fundamental reasons. First, Gonzalez still maintains
continuous personal contact with large numbers of his constituents. His
local office continues to receive a steady flow of daily visitors seeking advice and assistance; hundreds of letters are received each week
and he still personally signs the responses to each; almost every weekend he is back in San Antonio meeting with constituents and speaking to
local groups. The second reason for his position is the fact that, due to
redistricting, the Twentieth District is now comprised of the heart of
the City of San Antonio. This gives him a smaller geographic area to cover
and gives him a constituency composed predominantly of low to middle
income Mexican Americans, Anglos and Blacks. By and large, the Twentieth
Congressional District no longer contains large numbers of high income
residents.

Gonzalez' remarkable ability to gain favorable news media coverage
and his weekly visits to the District give him a commanding advantage.
His constituents have developed confidence in his ability to keep them
informed, serve their needs and represent their views. This personal
contact with constituents creates a positive relationship with the voters
that is extremely difficult for any prospective opponent to overcome.

Most observers would agree that Gonzalez has had considerable influence on local elections despite the fact that he does not actively support candidates in the Democratic Primary or city elections. An exception occurred in 1971 when he supported the local Good Government League candidates who were opposed by a handful of independents. His main target in this case was City Councilman Pete Torres who had openly and severely criticized Gonzalez' support of the Defense budget. Torres maintained that Gonzalez was supporting the bombings in Vietnam by voting for the Defense budget. The Congressman took the position that Torres' public opposition to the Defense budget was a major liability to the protection of the more than 20,000 jobs at Kelly Air Force Base and he should not be re-elected.

Protection of the civilian jobs at Kelly has been a major task for Gonzalez throughout his congressional career. Kelly Air Force Base is San Antonio's single largest employer and loss of these jobs would cause an economic catastrophe in the city. Torres experienced the full impact of Gonzalez' counterattack in defense of Kelly and lost the election by a substantial margin. There are some who attribute Gonzalez' abandonment of his traditionally neutral position as a deliberate act to demolish a potential challenger. While there could be some element of truth in this theory, there is ample evidence to support the "defense of jobs at Kelly" position.

In addition to protecting jobs at Kelly, Gonzalez has been active in obtaining grants and loans for numerous federal and local activities including a federal building complex, a Veterans Administration hospital and urban renewal, economic development, employment, school and housing programs. Those who are familiar with the federal budget process know that success in obtaining funds for local projects requires patience, diligence and hard work. All of the political and legislative skills of a congressman must be used. For example, major construction projects require initial justification and planning, construction and operating funds. At any point in the process a project can be jeopardized by accidental or deliberate actions. Nevertheless, even during two terms of a Republican Administration, Gonzalez has managed to "bring home the bacon" and fulfill a major portion of his original campaign platform. Consequently, most residents of San Antonio look to Gonzalez as a public official constantly on guard, protecting their interests at the federal level.

At the time the thesis was written, Gonzalez was implementing his HemisFair Project. In 1968, the Fair was held with official designation by the Bureau of International Expositions as a World Fair. A twelve-million-dollar convention center complex which was built with local and federal funds in preparation for the HemisFair has added to the city's competitive position in attracting tourist and convention trade, the area's second largest economic generator. While some local criticism was raised against governmental investment in HemisFair in lieu of development efforts in San Antonio's poverty pockets, most residents supported the World Fair project. A visible result of HemisFair is a significant growth in San Antonio's tourist trade. This has produced new jobs and improved the city's economic base.

Some observers contend that HemisFair is resulting in long range changes in San Antonio that are subtle yet real. Specifically, they say that before HemisFair, the city was controlled by a small group of provincial individuals who resisted new ideas and outside influences. HemisFair, in the eyes of these observers, gave others in San Antonio the opportunity to take part in leadership positions. More importantly, new ideas, new people and new outlooks on progress were allowed to exist. The fruits of this subtle influence are still being manifested, though many believe much too slowly.

Gonzalez' role in supporting Democratic candidates in the November General Elections is now traditionally accepted by candidates and voters. Every two years, Gonzalez embraces all the Democratic Party candidates and begins a personal barnstorming tour in their behalf. Flaying away at the non-Democratic candidates, he appears on television and radio, attends rallies, meetings and social gatherings, sends letters and holds press conferences for the Democrats. Candidates who have serious opponents receive special support from Gonzalez. For example, in 1972, when most Democratic officials were trying to avoid association with George McGovern, Gonzalez campaigned extensively for the Democratic presidential nominee. The Congressman's ability to deliver votes in his district can be measured, in part, by the election results. In the Twentieth District, McGovern received 61% of the votes for President.

Yet, if there is any single criticism that is heard most often about Gonzalez, it is that he does not support Mexican American candidates for office because he reputedly doesn't want any competition in his role as the leading political figure in the city. Undoubtedly, this criticism stems from Gonzalez' long standing policy of refusing to endorse candidates during the Democratic primary elections. Some individuals believe that with Gonzalez' endorsements many more Mexican Americans would be holding elective offices in San Antonio. The Congressman's refusal to endorse candidates in the primary or to get involved in intra-party battles has led to numerous disagreements with some local politicians and would-be office holders. The principal reason for these problems is either a failure to understand Gonzalez' policy or a refusal to accept the validity of his neutrality. Despite vocal criticism by some, Gonzalez' approach to local elections is accepted by the majority of his constituents.

A related area which has resulted in criticism of Gonzalez is his position on some of the protest actions by Chicano activists. As a visible symbol of one strategy for personal and group success, Gonzalez became a target for criticism by groups of militant activists who expressed impatience with gradual reforms and demanded immediate improvements in the conditions of La Raza (our people). In some instances, demonstrations were held to criticize him and disrupt meetings he was attending.

In turn, Gonzalez expressed his opposition to what he called "racism in reverse." Gonzalez maintained that some activists and their "hate the gringo" rhetoric were inflaming passions rather than solving problems. He said their aims were not to get equality, but "to get even." The debate resulted in widely publicized confrontations between Gonzalez and some activists.

Exercising his role as an educator of the public, Gonzalez again spoke out against the sin of racism. First it was the segregation bills in Texas, now it was those Chicano activists who were fanning flames of "hate the gringo." In his view, hatred among races and ethnic groups must be combated at all costs because of its ability to mortally infect civilizations. He believes that racism, no matter what its disguise, must not be allowed to exist. When he sees what he believes to be blatant racism, he strikes out against its perpetrators like Christ banishing the money changers from the temple. This reflects a basic consistency in Gonzalez that is often not recognized.

To a great extent, this consistency stems from a fundamental faith in the basic goodness of the people as a whole. A belief that, in the long run, the people will strive to do the greatest good for the greatest number in a spirit of equality and with respect for the rights of the minority. Any person or group who attempts to alter this natural inclination will be subjected to Gonzalez' wrath. In this case, it was certain Chicano activists and it resulted in the labeling of Gonzalez by some as a "conservative" and even worse, a "vendido" (sellout). Ironically, when he took an anti-racist position in the Texas Senate, he was labeled a left-wing liberal—the same man, the same belief, a different label. Certainly, from the social science perspective this confrontation bears need for further study and analysis to determine its place in the continuing development of America's Hispanic population.

The brevity and selectivity of these few comments on Gonzalez' performance during the last ten years illustrate the need to update his biography. Until this is done, the reader should recognize that the original work was written as a Master's Thesis in the study of American Government. While many changes have occurred since then, the basic thrust remains—Henry B. Gonzalez is a unique person who is totally committed to public service and has upset traditional definitions of success and power. His success and strength do not result from personal wealth or control of a powerful organization, but from an almost mystical belief in people and an unusual ability to maintain their trust, confidence and support. Although occasional voices of criticism have been raised against him, he remains a singularly popular elected official. As of this writing, he is running unopposed for re-election to his ninth term in Congress. Some supporters are even suggesting a campaign to draft Gonzalez for Vice President. Gonzalez replies that he is pleased with his legislative career and has no ambitions to change it. In fact, his public record shows a consistent approach to his work, a dedicated loyalty to his constituents and a fundamental belief in democracy. These are attributes which mark a true public servant, be he councilman, senator, congressman, or vice president.

March, 1976   E.R., Jr.

ABOUT THE AUTHOR

Eugene Rodriguez, Jr. was born on February 9, 1941 in San Antonio, Texas. He was graduated from Central Catholic High School in 1959 and received a Bachelor of Arts in Government from St. Mary's University in 1963. In 1965, he received a Master of Arts in Government from St. Mary's. His thesis was entitled Henry B. Gonzalez: A Political Profile.

Rodriguez' experience includes two years as a special assistant to Congressman Henry B. Gonzalez, two years active duty in the United States Army during which time he achieved the rank of Captain and was awarded the Army Commendation Medal for service in the Republic of South Korea. He has also served as Director of the Concentrated Employment Program, a manpower delivery system funded for over four million dollars annually to serve 3000 disadvantaged, unemployed persons. From 1970 to 1973, he was Executive Director of the Economic Opportunities Development Corporation (EODC), the ten million dollar Community Action Agency of San Antonio. He then moved to Washington, D.C. as Deputy Director, Field Operations for the National Urban Coalition, where he co-authored the Community Manpower Programming Handbook.

He is now engaged in independent management and community development consulting work in San Antonio. Mr. Rodriguez and his wife, Sylvia, are expecting their first child in July, 1976.

THE CHICANO HERITAGE

An Arno Press Collection

Adams, Emma H. **To and Fro in Southern California.** 1887

Anderson, Henry P. **The Bracero Program in California.** 1961

Aviña, Rose Hollenbaugh. **Spanish and Mexican Land Grants in California.** 1976

Barker, Ruth Laughlin. **Caballeros.** 1932

Bell, Horace. **On the Old West Coast.** 1930

Biberman, Herbert. **Salt of the Earth.** 1965

Casteñeda, Carlos E., trans. **The Mexican Side of the Texas Revolution (1836).** 1928

Casteñeda, Carlos E. **Our Catholic Heritage in Texas, 1519-1936.** Seven volumes. 1936-1958

Colton, Walter. **Three Years in California.** 1850

Cooke, Philip St. George. **The Conquest of New Mexico and California.** 1878

Cue Canovas, Agustin. **Los Estados Unidos Y El Mexico Olvidado.** 1970

Curtin, L. S. M. **Healing Herbs of the Upper Rio Grande.** 1947

Fergusson, Harvey. **The Blood of the Conquerors.** 1921

Fernandez, Jose. **Cuarenta Años de Legislador:** Biografia del Senador Casimiro Barela. 1911

Francis, Jessie Davies. **An Economic and Social History of Mexican California** (1822-1846). Volume I: Chiefly Economic. Two vols. in one. 1976

Getty, Harry T. **Interethnic Relationships in the Community of Tucson.** 1976

Guzman, Ralph C. **The Political Socialization of the Mexican American People.** 1976

Harding, George L. **Don Agustin V. Zamorano.** 1934

Hayes, Benjamin. **Pioneer Notes from the Diaries of Judge Benjamin Hayes, 1849-1875.** 1929

Herrick, Robert. **Waste.** 1924

Jamieson, Stuart. **Labor Unionism in American Agriculture.** 1945

Landolt, Robert Garland. **The Mexican-American Workers of San Antonio, Texas.** 1976

Lane, Jr., John Hart. **Voluntary Associations Among Mexican Americans in San Antonio, Texas.** 1976

Livermore, Abiel Abbot. **The War with Mexico Reviewed.** 1850

Loyola, Mary. **The American Occupation of New Mexico, 1821-1852.** 1939

Macklin, Barbara June. **Structural Stability and Culture Change in a Mexican-American Community.** 1976

McWilliams, Carey. **Ill Fares the Land:** Migrants and Migratory Labor in the United States. 1942

Murray, Winifred. **A Socio-Cultural Study of 118 Mexican Families Living in a Low-Rent Public Housing Project in San Antonio, Texas.** 1954

Niggli, Josephina. **Mexican Folk Plays.** 1938

Parigi, Sam Frank. **A Case Study of Latin American Unionization in Austin, Texas.** 1976

Poldervaart, Arie W. **Black-Robed Justice.** 1948

Rayburn, John C. and Virginia Kemp Rayburn, eds. **Century of Conflict, 1821-1913.** Incidents in the Lives of William Neale and William A. Neale, Early Settlers in South Texas. 1966

Read, Benjamin. **Illustrated History of New Mexico.** 1912

Rodriguez, Jr., Eugene. **Henry B. Gonzalez.** 1976

Sanchez, Nellie Van de Grift. **Spanish and Indian Place Names of California.** 1930

Sanchez, Nellie Van de Grift. **Spanish Arcadia.** 1929

Shulman, Irving. **The Square Trap.** 1953

Tireman, L. S. **Teaching Spanish-Speaking Children.** 1948

Tireman, L. S. and Mary Watson. **A Community School in a Spanish-Speaking Village.** 1948

Twitchell, Ralph Emerson. **The History of the Military Occupation of the Territory of New Mexico.** 1909

Twitchell, Ralph Emerson. **The Spanish Archives of New Mexico.** Two vols. 1914

U. S. House of Representatives. **California and New Mexico:** Message from the President of the United States, January 21, 1850. 1850

Valdes y Tapia, Daniel. **Hispanos and American Politics.** 1976

West, Stanley A. **The Mexican Aztec Society.** 1976

Woods, Frances Jerome. **Mexican Ethnic Leadership in San Antonio, Texas.** 1949